PREDICTING THE MARKETS
TOPICAL STUDY #5

The Fed and
The Great Virus Crisis

Edward Yardeni
Melissa Tagg

YRI PRESS

Predicting the Markets Topical Study #5:
The Fed and The Great Virus Crisis

ISBN: 978-1-948025-16-4 (hardcover)
ISBN: 978-1-948025-10-2 (paperback)
ISBN: 978-1-948025-11-9 (eBook)
Library of Congress Control Number: 2021904248

The author has taken all reasonable steps to provide accurate information in this publication. However, no representation or warranty is made as to the fairness, accuracy, completeness, or correctness of the information and opinions contained herein. Over time, the statements made in this publication may no longer be accurate, true, or otherwise correct. Over time, the author's opinions as articulated in this publication may change. This publication should not be relied on for investment, accounting, legal, or other professional advice. If readers desire such advice, they should consult with a qualified professional. Nothing in this publication—including predictions, forecasts, and estimates for any and all markets—should be construed as recommendations to buy, sell or hold any security, including mutual funds, futures contracts, exchange-traded funds, or any other financial instruments.

Published by YRI Books, a division of Yardeni Research, Inc.
68 Wheatley Road, Suite 1100
Brookville, NY USA 11545

Contact us: **requests@yardeni.com**

Excerpted, updated, and expanded from *Predicting the Markets: A Professional Autobiography* (2018).

For our children

Melissa, Sarah, Samuel, David, and Laura Yardeni
&
Cecelia and Josephine Tagg

*Don't fight the Fed, especially
when the Fed is fighting a pandemic!*

Author's Note

This study is another in a series of Topical Studies examining issues that I discussed in my book *Predicting the Markets: A Professional Autobiography* (2018) but in greater detail and on a more current basis. Previous studies in this series, which are available on my Amazon homepage, include:

S&P 500 Earnings, Valuation, and the Pandemic (2020)

Fed Watching for Fun and Profit (2020)

Stock Buybacks: The True Story (2019)

The Yield Curve: What Is It Really Predicting? (2019)

The charts at the end of this study were current as of January 23, 2021. They are available in color along with linked endnotes and appendices at **www.yardenibook.com/studies**.

Institutional investors are invited to sign up for the Yardeni Research service on a complimentary trial basis at **www.yardeni.com/trial-registration**.

Contents

"The asset purchases that we're doing are a multiple of the programs that were done during the last crisis. . . . I will say that we're not out of ammunition by a long shot. No, there's really no limit to what we can do with these lending programs that we have. So, there's a lot more we can do to support the economy, and we're committed to doing everything we can as long as we need to."

—Federal Reserve Chair Jerome Powell
May 17, 2020

"We're not thinking about raising rates. We're not even thinking about thinking about raising rates."

—Federal Reserve Chair Jerome Powell
June 10, 2020

"By contrast, the risks of overdoing it seem, for now, to be smaller. Even if policy actions ultimately prove to be greater than needed, they will not go to waste. The recovery will be stronger and move faster if monetary policy and fiscal policy continue to work side by side to provide support to the economy until it is clearly out of the woods."

—Federal Reserve Chair Jerome Powell
October 6, 2020

Introduction

Irony of History

The word "irony" comes from the Greek word *eiron*, which was a stock character in ancient Greek theater. The eiron was the clever underdog who perpetually triumphed against all odds over his boastful opponent, the *alazon*. The ancient Greek playwrights' great sense of irony permeates their comedies and tragedies about the rise and fall of great men and women. For them, comedy and tragedy were the opposite ends of the same spectrum of the human condition.

On March 13, 2020, I published my book *Fed Watching for Fun and Profit*.[1] It was a depressing time. The World Health Organization (WHO) had just declared the Covid-19 pandemic on Wednesday, March 11. The following week, state governors started imposing lockdown restrictions to slow the spread of the virus. Even though I am an economist, not a virologist, I wished that instead of writing a book about the Federal Reserve, I had spent all that time researching and writing about viruses. That would have been a much more interesting and successful book under the circumstances.

Two weeks later, my book sales picked up significantly after the Fed responded to the financial and economic calamity resulting from the pandemic with a shock-and-awe program of ultra-easy monetary policies on Monday, March 23. The Fed's policy response to the Great Virus Crisis (GVC) of 2020 was much more shockingly awesome than any of the programs unleashed by the

Fed in response to the Great Financial Crisis (GFC) of 2008 and its aftermath.

Many aspects of the GVC have held ironies as rich as any penned by Aristophanes. For example, as I noted in *Fed Watching*, "Contrarians were put on high alert at the end of June 2017, when Fed Chair Janet Yellen said at a London conference: 'Would I say there will never, ever be another financial crisis? You know probably that would be going too far, but I do think we're much safer, and I hope it will not be in our lifetimes, and I don't believe it will be.'" When I heard that, I climbed out on a limb to predict that there would be another financial crisis in our lifetimes. I added, "However, like previous ones, it likely will offer a great opportunity for buying stocks."[2]

Ironically, I finished writing that book in late 2019, just weeks before the pandemic that would trigger exactly such a buying opportunity for stocks began to grip the world. *Fed Watching* covers the period from the Federal Reserve System's creation by the Federal Reserve Act, passed on December 13, 1913 through the end of 2019.

In the Epilogue of *Fed Watching*, I focused on the future of monetary policy. I observed that the world's major central banks have tried numerous unconventional policies to boost inflation and stimulate faster economic growth, including zero and negative interest-rate policies (ZIRP and NIRP), quantitative easing programs (QE), and ultra-easy forward guidance. These unconventional tools have become all too conventional since the GFC.

I asked, "So what's next?" I suggested that central banks might opt for "helicopter money" during the next crisis. The major central bankers might even embrace Modern Monetary Theory (MMT), I opined, as they increasingly acknowledged that monetary policy might be reaching the outer limits of its power and that it was time for fiscal policy to either take over or at least supplement monetary policy.

The Fed's response to the GFC was widely compared to fighting a war with bazookas. The concept was first introduced by Treasury Secretary Henry M. Paulson, Jr., when he told a congressional panel in July 2008 about his plans to stabilize the financial markets: "If you've got a bazooka, and people know you've got it, you may not have to take it out." As events unfolded, most of the firepower used to fight the GFC actually came from the Fed. However, when the GVC first started, it was widely perceived that the Fed had run out of ammo for the bazookas. Ironically and surprisingly, the Fed responded to the GVC with much more than helicopter money. It seemed to me that the Fed's shock-and-awe attack on the pandemic was more like carpet-bombing the financial markets and economy with cash dropped from B-52 bombers. Clearly, by doing so, the Fed, along with the other major central banks, demonstrated that they still had plenty of ammo and even more powerful weapons.

Ironically, while the central bankers demonstrated that they had a lot more firepower, they all pleaded for the fiscal policy authorities to join the fight against the GVC. In other words, the Fed and the other major central banks fully embraced MMT—which, ironically, isn't modern, isn't monetary, and isn't a theory. It's really a controversial proposition that a government that borrows in its own currency and can print that currency at will can also deficit-finance its spending at will without limit—unless and until doing so stimulates runaway inflation. According to MMT's proponents, the central bank can help grease the wheels by purchasing some or all of the resulting government debt and by keeping interest rates low—if inflation remains subdued.

Ironically, Fed Chair Jerome Powell hated the idea in early 2019, but he became its biggest proponent and enabler just one year later. In his semi-annual congressional testimony on monetary policy on Tuesday, February 26, 2019, he was asked about MMT and proceeded to rip it to shreds: "The idea that deficits don't matter for countries that can borrow in their own currency I think is just wrong." The "US debt is fairly high to the level of GDP—and much more importantly—it's growing faster than GDP, fairly significantly faster. We are going to have to spend less or raise more revenue."[3]

At the time, the annual deficit was on course to top $1 trillion in the coming years, according to the Congressional Budget Office (CBO). Powell added, "In addition to the extent that people are talking about using the Fed—our role is not to provide support for particular policies." He concluded, "Decisions about spending, and controlling spending and paying for it, are really for you." He was still strongly defending the Fed's independence and reiterating the Fed has no business commenting on, let alone supporting, fiscal policy. In effect, he told Congress: "Fiscal policy is your domain. Leave us out of it."

What a difference a pandemic makes, as this study will show in yet another irony of history!

With the benefit of hindsight, a better title for *Fed Watching* might have been *"Don't Fight the Fed!"* This sequel—which I've coauthored with Melissa Tagg, my colleague at Yardeni Research, Inc.—covers the Fed's extraordinary response to the GVC from the start of 2020 to the end of that year. Our basic theme is: "Don't fight the Fed, especially when the Fed is fighting a pandemic!"

Chapter 1
Great Virus Crisis

Calm Before the Storm

The year 2019 ended with lots of forecasters claiming 20-20 vision for the year 2020 just ahead. It was likely to be another year of growth for the economy, as 2019's trade tensions with China had eased thanks to a trade agreement at the start of 2020.

The economic expansion, which started during June 2009 according to the Dating Committee of the National Bureau of Economic Research (NBER), became the longest one on record during July 2019, when it turned 121 months old. The widespread consensus was that it would continue well into 2020 and possibly beyond. It ended during February 2020, when the Index of Coincident Economic Indicators (CEI) peaked at a record high following 128 months of expansion (*Fig. 1*).

Gross Domestic Product (GDP) is the broadest measure of national economic activity. It is available quarterly. On an inflation-adjusted basis, "real" GDP is highly correlated with the monthly CEI. A common definition of a recession is two consecutive quarterly declines in real GDP. Sure enough, it dropped 5.0% during the first quarter of 2020 and plunged 31.4% during the second quarter. Both numbers are reported on a seasonally adjusted annual rate (saar) basis.

The Federal Open Market Committee (FOMC) sets the Fed's monetary policy including the key federal funds interest rate. The committee meets eight times a year. The Summary of Economic Projections (SEP) released by the FOMC on December 11, 2019 showed that the median forecast of the FOMC's participants for real GDP in 2020 was 2.0%, down a bit from 2.2% during 2019. The Fed's policymaking committee had lowered the federal funds rate target three times during 2019 from a range of 2.25%-2.50% in the middle of the year to 1.50%-1.75% by the end of the year. The SEP showed the median federal funds rate forecast was 1.60% for 2020, unchanged from 2019. The core inflation rate, i.e., the headline rate excluding food and energy prices, was expected to tick up from 1.6% to 1.9%, while the unemployment rate was predicted to edge down from 3.6% to 3.5%.[4]

In other words, at the end of 2019, the FOMC expected continued economic growth without a recession in the year ahead. The unemployment rate was expected to stay near record lows, while inflation was expected to remain subdued.

One year later, the FOMC's December 16, 2020 SEP showed real GDP falling 3.7% in 2020 with the unemployment rate at 7.6% and inflation at 1.5%. The federal funds rate had been lowered to 0.00%–0.25% on March 15 and was expected to remain near zero through 2023 (*Fig. 2*). (See Appendix 1: FOMC Summary of Economic Projections.)

What a difference a pandemic makes!

Before the viral storm spread worldwide, there wasn't much to worry about. Indeed, our January 6, 2020 *Morning Briefing* was titled "Nothing to Fear But Nothing to Fear (and Iran)."[5] Iran's Mullahs were widely expected to retaliate against the US for assassinating their top general, Qassem Soleimani, on January 3 near the Baghdad International Airport.

With short-term and long-term interest rates expected to remain low in 2020, many investors continued to reach for yield, as evidenced by historically low credit-quality yield spreads in the bond market. Investors continued to buy stocks. They became excited by the latest product offerings at the Consumer Electronics

Show in Las Vegas at the beginning of 2020. A handful of Growth companies in the S&P 500 continued to outperform other stocks, as they had since 2017. In addition, stock investors reaching for yield continued to be attracted to stocks with dividend yields exceeding the 10-year US Treasury bond yield.

Also, at the beginning of 2020, in his January 4 American Economic Association Presidential Address, former Fed Chair Ben Bernanke questioned the notion that central bankers have "run out of room" to ease monetary policy if necessary. While the Fed may not have much room for "conventional" interest-rate cuts, he said, newer tools could be useful.

Bernanke's own new research showed quantitative easing (QE) programs to be effective even when interest rates were as low as zero. Moreover, bond purchases should not be viewed as a last resort for central bankers but part of "the standard toolkit," he said. According to Bernanke, a combination of QE and forward guidance by the Fed could produce "the equivalent of about three additional percentage points of short-term rate cuts." In other words, the Fed had plenty of "policy space."[6]

The same day, January 4, Bernanke shared his views in a panel discussion alongside former Fed Chair Janet Yellen and current Fed Chair Jerome Powell.[7] Yellen agreed that the Fed's tools "were effective, should remain in the toolkit, and potentially can be strengthened." Powell, clearly valuing the opinions of his predecessors, said: "I would agree with . . . both Ben and Janet . . . that the tools that we used in the crisis after hitting the zero lower bound generally worked. . . . [We'll] use all of our tools to the extent appropriate. We'll use the balance sheet. We'll use the tools that we have."

In a January 9 interview on Bloomberg Television's *Wall Street Week,* former Treasury Secretary Lawrence Summers dismissed Bernanke's optimism. He derided Bernanke's speech as "a kind of last hurrah for the central bankers." He added that it's "pretty unlikely" that the Fed would lower interest rates by as much again "given that in recessions we usually cut interest rates by five percentage points and interest rates today are below two percent." Summers added, "I just don't believe QE and that stuff is worth anything like another three percentage points." He said, "We're going to have to rely on putting money in people's pockets, on direct government spending."[8] As we will see, Summers was half right.

According to the minutes of the last FOMC meeting of 2019, on December 10–11, the committee's participants "discussed how maintaining the current stance of policy for a time could be helpful for cushioning the economy from the global developments that have been weighing on economic activity."[9] They were mostly concerned about global economic weakness and geopolitical matters, especially mounting trade tensions between the US and China. At his press conference after the meeting, Powell said that he'd like to see persistent upward momentum in inflation before raising interest rates again.[10]

On January 15, 2020, the US and China signed a trade deal, with China agreeing to purchase more US goods and services and to provide greater access for American firms to China's financial sector. However, the US didn't get the fundamental reforms in Chinese economic policy to help American businesses that it had sought. And US tariffs remained on about $370 billion of Chinese exports.

That was the calm before the storm.

The Twilight Zone

Ironically, our Wednesday, January 22, 2020 *Morning Briefing* was titled "Happy Chinese New Year."[11] We wrote, "Last year was the

Year of the Pig in the Chinese Zodiac. It wasn't a good year for pigs. The swine flu decimated China's hog population in 2019. . . . This year is the Year of the Rat. This rodent has a long history of spreading diseases." We were reacting to some news that had just started coming out of China about a virus outbreak.

Friday of that same week, on January 24, the S&P 500 dropped 0.9% on fear that the coronavirus outbreak in China was spreading rapidly and could turn into a pandemic. Our Monday, January 27, 2020 *Morning Briefing* was titled "Going Viral."[12] We wrote:

> What's the difference between an epidemic and a pandemic? The former occurs when a disease either affects more people than usual within a locality or spreads beyond its usual locality. A pandemic is an epidemic of worldwide proportions. The recent coronavirus outbreak has the potential to turn into a pandemic since it has already spread beyond China's borders.

That same day, the S&P 500 plunged 1.6%. The most unsettling news over the weekend was that people infected with the virus might show no symptoms for two weeks but still can be contagious during that time. That was not the case during the Severe Acute Respiratory Syndrome (SARS) viral outbreak of 2003 in China, which was quickly contained.

Monday's steep decline in stock prices around the world reflected mounting fear that China's epidemic was turning into a full-blown global pandemic as the number of cases rose in Iran, Italy, and South Korea over the weekend. That same day, the price of copper moved lower, while the price of gold rose to a seven-year high (*Fig. 3*). The yield-curve spread between the federal funds rate and the 10-year US Treasury bond yield turned negative, falling to –21 basis points from a recent high of 38 basis points. Such an "inversion" of the yield curve has signaled recessions in the past.

The news coming out of China was increasingly alarming. To stop the coronavirus outbreak, nearly 60 million people in the city of Wuhan and surrounding Hubei province were placed under quarantine. Workers who visited family there over the Lunar New Year holiday couldn't return home to work. And travelers returning home from elsewhere in China were required to self-quarantine for 14 days.

Meanwhile, an estimated five million people had left Wuhan, either in anticipation of the quarantine or to be with family during the Lunar New Year holiday, which had been extended beyond the traditional one-week celebration period to two weeks. Foreign governments airlifted their citizens out of Wuhan and placed them in isolation for 14 days, which was believed to be how long it takes for the virus' symptoms to show up. Apple shut its stores on the Chinese mainland. So did Ikea. By the start of February, many countries had banned flights in and out of China. Russia closed its border with China. Deaths were soaring in China.

In late January, deaths were starting to soar outside of China. South Korea counted six dead from the coronavirus and more than 600 infected. Italy had seen two deaths and 100 confirmed cases of the virus. Lombardy and Veneto were under strict quarantine; no one could enter or leave these administrative regions for the next two weeks without special permission. Beyond the quarantined zones, many businesses, schools, sports games, and events in Italy, including the Venice Carnival, were suspended or cancelled. In the Middle East, Iran's borders were closed, and flights into the country stopped.

The S&P 500 stock price index peaked at 3329.62 on Friday, January 17. It then fell 3.1% through the last day of January on pandemic fears. However, the index then proceeded to rally 5.0% to a record high of 3386.15 through Wednesday, February 19. It plunged again, by 3.0%, on Tuesday, February 25 after an official at the US Centers for Disease Control and Prevention (CDC) that day said Americans should prepare for Covid-19 to spread in their communities. "We really want to prepare the American public for the possibility that their lives will be disrupted because of this pandemic," Dr. Nancy Messonnier, director of the CDC's National Center for Immunization and Respiratory Diseases, told reporters. She said that Americans should talk to their children's schools about contingency education and childcare plans and discuss tele-working options at work if community spread is reported in the US.[13]

When asked by a reporter on a conference call whether her tone had changed compared to previous calls, the CDC official said: "The data over the last week and the spread in other countries has certainly raised our level of concern and raised our level of expectation that we are going to have community spread here. . . . That's why we are asking folks in every sector as well as within their families to start planning for this." Messonnier said that she spoke to her family over breakfast on that Tuesday, and that while she believed the risk of catching coronavirus at that time was low, she told them they needed to be preparing for "significant disruption" to their lives.

On Wednesday, March 11, 2020, the WHO officially declared that the Covid-19 pandemic had spread all around the world. The declaration precipitated the GVC as governments around the world locked down their economies to slow the spread of the virus. The result was a severe global recession. (See Appendix 2: A Timeline of the Covid-19 Pandemic, 2020.)

On Monday, March 16, President Donald Trump pivoted from saying that Covid-19 was like a bad flu to warning that Americans should stay home if state governors issued orders to do so. That was the gist of the new guidelines issued by the White House that day "for every American to follow over the next 15 days as we combat the virus." The governor of California issued a stay-in-place order on March 19; New York's governor followed on March 20, and the rest of the states' governors did the same over the following few days.

Businesses closed. Everyone stayed home. The streets were empty. It was like being in the Twilight Zone. Ironically, the very first episode of *The Twilight Zone*, which aired on CBS on October 2, 1959, was titled "Where Is Everybody?"[14] The TV series was created by Rod Serling and broadcast from 1959 to 1964. Each episode started with Serling explaining: "There is a fifth dimension, beyond that which is known to man. It is a dimension as vast as space and as timeless as infinity. It is the middle ground between light and shadow, between science and superstition, and it lies between the pit of man's fears and the summit of his knowledge. This is the dimension of imagination. It is an area which we call 'The Twilight Zone.'"

That is a remarkably good description of the predicament that humankind confronted during the GVC.

In *The Twilight Zone*, fear is the all-consuming emotion that often leads to madness. On February 26, two weeks before the WHO's pandemic declaration and when the S&P 500 closed at 3116.39, we wrote that "extreme government responses aimed at containing the virus, while effective, will create a pandemic of fear, increasing the risk of a global recession and a bear market in stocks."[15] On March 10, we wrote: "The pandemic of fear continues to spread faster than the cause of that fear, namely, the Covid-19 virus."[16]

Global oil demand was hit hard by the pandemic. A resulting price war between Saudi Arabia and Russia caused the price of a barrel of Brent crude oil to plunge 24% from $45.35 on Friday, March 6 to $34.50 on Monday, March 9 (*Fig. 4*). A much bigger, 76%, plunge in the price of oil during the second half of 2014 through early 2016 caused high-yield, credit-quality yield spreads to widen dramatically as yields on energy-related junk bonds soared relative to US Treasury bond yields. However, this time, they widened significantly in a matter of a few days instead of months, as occurred during the 2015 episode.

This time, investment-grade corporate yield spreads widened rapidly as well. The yield spread between AAA-rated municipal bonds and the 10-year US Treasury bond also widened ominously as investors started to worry that state and local tax revenues would be depressed.

We started to monitor what we called the "mad dash for cash."[17] Everyone seemed to want to get out of everything at the same time to raise cash. Individual investors indiscriminately sold their bond mutual funds and exchange-traded funds (ETFs). That caused the credit markets to freeze up. By the market close of Thursday, March 12, the S&P 500 had plunged 26.7% from its February 19 record high. Even Treasury bond yields moved higher, while the price of gold dropped by $83.05 per ounce to $1,570.70.

The financial system seemed to be on the verge of imploding during the GVC just as it had during the GFC.

Chapter 2
Fed Goes to War

Fed's B-52 Bombers

As noted above, the S&P 500 peaked at a then-record high of 3386.15 on February 19. That day, our *Morning Briefing* coincidentally was titled "In a Good Place?"[18]

After reading the Federal Reserve's 71-page semi-annual *Monetary Policy Report* (MPR) to Congress dated February 7, 2020, we had concluded that Fed officials believed the US economy was well balanced and that, therefore, they would keep the federal funds rate in the current range of 1.50%–1.75%.[19] Nevertheless, they were concerned about several global issues, which they were monitoring closely, including the epidemic in China.

Federal Reserve Chair Jerome Powell emphasized during his congressional testimony, discussing the report on February 11 and February 12, that the "US economy is in a very good place." The threat from the coronavirus was something to watch, he said, but too early to understand. Nevertheless, he affirmed that "there is no reason why the expansion can't continue." Most of the issues discussed in the *MPR* had been around since the current expansion began. The two new developments were trade tensions, which started in 2018 but had recently diminished, and the coronavirus, which had been a global risk to health, economic growth, and stock markets only since the start of 2020.[20]

Powell first used the expression "in a good place" referring to inflation during his September 26, 2018 press conference.[21] In his January 30, 2019 press conference, he said, "The US economy is in a good place."[22] He used "in a good place" to describe the economy and Fed policy four times during his March 20, 2019 press conference.[23] The four-word phrase appeared again at the following pressers: May 1, 2019 (once), June 19, 2019 (thrice), July 31, 2019 (once), September 18, 2019 (none), October 30, 2019 (thrice), and December 11, 2019 (once). At his first presser of the new year on January 29, 2020, he said that "household debt is in a good place, a very good place."[24]

In his February 11, 2020 testimony, Powell upgraded his assessment of the US economy as being in a "very good place." On February 19, the same day the market peaked as it was about to crater, we wrote: "We wish he would stop using that expression. Our contrary instincts come out every time he says it."

In any event, the *MPR* did mention the virus development eight times, including, "More recently, possible spillovers from the effects of the coronavirus in China have presented a new risk to the outlook," and, "The recent emergence of the coronavirus . . . could lead to disruptions in China that spill over to the rest of the global economy." Nevertheless, the *MPR* implied that Fed officials expected this virus outbreak, like previous ones, to pass before long without overly disrupting the US economy.

In a February 20 CNBC interview, Fed Vice Chair Richard Clarida reiterated that the "fundamentals in the US are strong," though he said Fed officials are monitoring risks, in particular the coronavirus. "It's obviously something that is probably going to have a noticeable impact on Chinese growth in the first quarter," he said. However, he dismissed expectations that the Fed will be cutting the federal funds rate anytime soon, implying that China's health crisis should be contained without having much impact on the US economy.[25]

The rally in the bond market at the time suggested that investors begged to differ and were discounting a rate cut by the Fed before long. Since January 23 (the day before the outbreak made headlines) through February 21, the 10-year US Treasury bond yield had declined by 28 basis points from 1.74% to 1.46%. Stock prices, coincidently, had been making record highs almost on a daily basis through February 19 on expectations that either the global health crisis would end soon or the Fed and the other major central banks would inject more liquidity into global financial markets to fight the adverse economic consequences of a prolonged crisis.

On Friday, February 28 at 2:30 p.m., Powell issued the following terse and unusual statement: "The fundamentals of the U.S. economy remain strong. However, the coronavirus poses evolving risks to economic activity. The Federal Reserve is closely monitoring developments and their implications for the economic outlook. We will use our tools and act as appropriate to support the economy."[26]

Consequently, another round of Fed rate-cutting was widely anticipated imminently. In our Monday, March 2 *Morning Briefing* titled "The Plot Sickens," we wrote that "the markets are expecting that the federal funds rate will be lowered by 100 basis points over the next 12 months. The surprise is that it could all happen as a one-shot rate cut."[27] On Tuesday, March 3, in an emergency session, the FOMC voted to cut the federal funds rate by 50 basis points, bringing it down to a range of 1.00%–1.25%.[28] The committee was widely expected to cut the rate again when the FOMC was scheduled to meet on Wednesday, March 18, by as much as 100 basis points to a range of 0.00%-0.25%, i.e., back to the "effective lower bound."

On Friday, March 6, Boston Fed President Eric Rosengren suggested that it was time to change the Federal Reserve Act to "allow the central bank to purchase a broader range of securities or assets." Rosengren also called on fiscal policy to do more.[29] The Trump administration was considering tax cuts, which would boost consumers' income but also bloat the already bloated federal budget deficit. In our Thursday, March 12 *Morning Briefing* titled "Fear for All," we wrote that we wouldn't be surprised if President Trump and Fed Chair Jerome Powell agreed to implement so-called "helicopter money." Fiscal policy would cut taxes, and monetary policy would buy the Treasury bonds issued to finance the fiscal stimulus.[30]

On Sunday evening, March 15, in another emergency session, the FOMC slashed the federal funds rate by 100 basis points to a range of 0.00%–0.25%. The Federal Reserve Board of Governors slashed the discount rate from 1.50% to 0.25%, and bank reserve requirements were dropped to zero.[31]

In addition, bond purchases would resume. It would be QE4, the fourth round of such purchases since the GFC.[32] The Fed would increase its holdings of Treasury securities by at least $500 billion and its holdings of agency mortgage-backed securities (MBS) by at least $200 billion. Unlike previous QE programs, no monthly schedule of purchases was set. Presumably, the Fed would purchase securities as deemed necessary to provide liquidity to the financial markets.[33]

That same day, the Bank of Canada, the Bank of England, the Bank of Japan, the European Central Bank, the Federal Reserve, and the Swiss National Bank announced a coordinated action to enhance the provision of liquidity via the standing US dollar liquidity swap line arrangements.[34]

The prior week's liquidity crisis in the capital markets certainly spooked Fed officials as much as it spooked investors. The Fed measures would pour more liquidity into the financial markets and were expected to help stabilize them by calming the pandemic of fear.

Instead, stock markets fell sharply around the world on Monday despite the Fed's easing announcements on Sunday. The

S&P 500 dropped 12.0%. One obvious conclusion was that the Fed's unconventional policies had become all too conventional and lost their effectiveness. The markets' adverse reaction to the Fed's moves suggested that the Fed no longer had the firepower to shock and awe.

Then again, Monday's selloff might have been caused by Sunday evening's viral rumors, primarily spread through text messages on social media, that President Trump was going to announce a mandatory two-week quarantine for the whole country. An alarming message warned: "Please be advised. Within 48 to 72 hours the President will evoke what is called the Stafford Act. Stock up on whatever you guys need to make sure you have a two-week supply of everything. Please forward to your network." The White House debunked the rumor in a tweet, saying "Text message rumors of a national #quarantine are FAKE. There is no national lockdown."[35]

Nevertheless, on Monday, President Trump did change his mind about the pandemic. As recently as Sunday, Trump was telling Americans to "relax," the pandemic would pass. On Monday, he pivoted from cheerleader-in-chief to commander-in-chief. In effect, he conceded that we were at war with the virus that caused the disease: "We have an invisible enemy." He acknowledged that the virus is extremely contagious, saying: "This is a bad one. This is a very bad one." At a news conference on Monday, Trump released his guidelines that called for people to avoid gathering in groups of more than 10 people; refrain from eating and drinking at bars, restaurants, and food courts; and work or attend school from home whenever possible.

Apparently, Dr. Anthony Fauci, director of the National Institute of Allergy and Infectious Diseases, had finally managed to convince the President that he had to do everything in his power to flatten the curve of infections, thus lowering the stress on the hospital system by reducing the numbers of cases and deaths. Administration officials, including the President, had been spooked by alarming predictive models forecasting that deaths would soar without more aggressive and universal social-distancing measures.

In our Tuesday, March 17 *Morning Briefing*, we concluded that the Fed would have to do more. We wrote that we wouldn't be surprised if the Fed asked Congress for authorization to purchase corporate bonds. We also predicted that the Fed was likely to revive some of the liquidity programs that worked quite well in 2008 and 2009, especially the commercial paper facility that injected liquidity into that distressed market.[36]

Sure enough, that very same day the Fed announced the reopening of the Primary Dealer Credit Facility (PDCF). It allowed primary dealers to offer credit via both overnight and term funding with maturities up to 90 days, which would support smooth market functioning.[37] In addition, the Fed announced that it would reopen the Commercial Paper Funding Facility (CPFF) to provide a liquidity backstop to US issuers of commercial paper through a special purpose vehicle (SPV) that would purchase unsecured and asset-backed commercial paper rated A1/P1 directly from eligible companies. Both facilities were first established in response to the GFC.

The CPFF program was established by the Fed under the authority of Section 13(3) of the Federal Reserve Act, with approval of the Treasury secretary. The Treasury would provide $10 billion of credit protection to the Fed in connection with the CPFF from the Treasury's Exchange Stabilization Fund (ESF). In turn, the Fed would then provide financing to the SPV under the CPFF. Its loans would be secured by the assets of the SPV.[38]

On Wednesday, March 18, a similar SPV, funded by the Treasury with up to $10 billion in credit protection to the Fed, was reopened to support money market mutual funds. Through the Money Market Mutual Fund Liquidity Facility (MMLF), the Federal Reserve Bank of Boston would make loans available to eligible financial institutions secured by high-quality assets purchased by the financial institution from money market mutual funds.[39] The MMLF was yet another GFC-legacy liquidity facility.

On Friday, March 20, the MMLF program was expanded to support the municipal credit market. The Federal Reserve Bank of Boston would be able to make loans available to eligible financial institutions secured by certain high-quality assets purchased from single-state and other tax-exempt municipal money market mutual funds.[40]

My advice to investors in our March 17 morning commentary was "Don't panic." I wrote, "I do think it is too late to panic, but I'm not sure. That's because predicting the pandemic of fear is harder than predicting the pandemic of the virus fueling the fear, as the former is spreading much faster than the latter. Perversely, the more fear the better, because the best cure for a viral pandemic is a viral panic. . . ."[41]

The panic ended on Tuesday, March 24, the day after the Fed expanded QE4 into what we dubbed "QE4ever." In our March 25 *Morning Briefing*, we stated that Monday might have made the low in this bear market.[42] So, just one week after QE4 was introduced, it morphed into QE4ever. The Fed would buy securities "in the amounts needed to support smooth market functioning and effective transmission of monetary policy to broader financial conditions and the economy." There would be no set purchasing schedule, no upper limit, and no end date. The program included purchases of agency commercial MBS in addition to Treasuries and residential MBS. The Open Market Desk at the Federal Reserve Bank of New York was instructed to continue offering large-scale overnight and term repurchase agreement operations.[43]

The Treasury committed another $30 billion from its Exchange Stabilization Fund to the Fed for it to establish up to $300 billion worth of new financing programs. This allowed the Fed to support the corporate sector without needing to get congressional authorization to purchase corporate bonds. The Fed established two brand new liquidity facilities to support credit to large employers: the Primary Market Corporate Credit Facility (PMCCF) for new bond and loan issuance and the Secondary Market Corporate Credit Facility (SMCCF) to provide liquidity for outstanding corporate bonds. The former was open to investment-grade companies and would provide bridge financing of four years. The latter would purchase in the secondary market corporate bonds issued by investment-grade US companies as well as US-listed ETFs designed with an investment objective of providing broad exposure to the market for US investment-grade corporate bonds.

The March 27 *Wall Street Journal* reported: "Under its governing law, the Fed can't directly buy corporate debt, and it is limited to purchasing municipal debt of six months or less. But it can work around these restrictions by creating lending facilities that lend or purchase debt, subject to approval of the Treasury secretary. . . . Over two weeks, the Fed has unveiled six lending facilities, five of them enjoying a total of $50 billion in support from the Treasury."[44]

The March 23 program added a sixth liquidity facility, the Term Asset-Backed Securities Loan Facility (TALF), to enable the issuance of asset-backed securities secured by student loans, auto loans, credit card loans, loans guaranteed by the Small Business Administration (SBA), and certain other assets. It was also a GFC-legacy facility. Both the MMLF and the CPFF were expanded to provide additional support to the municipal credit markets. Finally, the Fed's March 23 press release stated that the Fed expected soon to announce the establishment of a Main Street Lending

Program (MSLP) to support lending to eligible small and medium-sized businesses, complementing efforts by the SBA.

These measures immediately improved liquidity in the credit markets; they no longer were frozen. The lender of last resort stood ready to be the buyer of last resort in the credit markets. Institutional managers of balanced funds rushed to sell their bonds and used the cash to rebalance into equities. The S&P 500, which had plunged 33.9% from February 19 through March 23, soared 13.6% through Friday, March 27.

During the GFC of 2008, Fed officials had to scramble to set up liquidity facilities to deal with a cascading credit crunch. It was as though the Fed was playing Whac-A-Mole in the credit system. So it was again: Revival and expansion of the GFC-era facilities allowed the Fed to fend off a GVC-induced credit crunch. But this time, these facilities were expanded to facilitate the flow of credit not just to businesses but also to municipalities, which were facing enormous declines in their tax revenues.

In addition, the Fed had cut the federal funds rate, the discount rate, and bank reserve requirements. It had expanded central bank liquidity swap lines. The March 23 press release concluded:

> Taken together, these actions will provide support to a wide range of markets and institutions, thereby supporting the flow of credit in the economy. The Federal Reserve will continue to use its full range of tools to support the flow of credit to households and businesses and thereby promote its maximum employment and price stability goals.

That turned out to be an understatement. And there was more to come. Indeed, on April 9, the Fed issued a press release headlined "Federal Reserve takes additional actions to provide up to $2.3 trillion in loans to support the economy."[45] That was made possible by the Coronavirus Aid, Relief, and Economic Security (CARES)

Act, which was signed by President Donald Trump on March 27. It provided the Treasury with $454 billion in capital for the Fed to leverage into around $4 trillion in loans through its various liquidity facilities.

Two additional facilities were established. The Paycheck Protection Program Liquidity Facility (PPPLF) would extend credit to eligible financial institutions that originated loans under the Paycheck Protection Program (PPP), taking the loans as collateral at face value. The PPP was created under the CARES Act to encourage employers to maintain their payrolls with the benefit of forgivable loans from the government. The new Municipal Liquidity Facility (MLF) would offer up to $500 billion in lending to states and municipalities. The Treasury would provide $35 billion of credit protection to the Federal Reserve for the MLF using funds appropriated by the CARES Act.

The April 9 press release announced the expansion of the size and scope of the PMCCF and SMCCF as well as the TALF. These three programs would now support up to $850 billion in credit backed by $85 billion in credit protection provided by the Treasury. The MSLP was projected to purchase up to $600 billion in loans, backed by $75 billion provided by the Treasury through the CARES Act. (See Appendix 3: The Fed's Liquidity Facilities, 2020.)

A billion here, a billion there adds up to serious money.

The Fed continued to expand its holdings of Treasuries and MBS under QE4ever. Altogether, they increased $2.9 trillion from the last week of February through the last week of 2020 to a record high of $6.8 trillion (*Fig. 5*). To track the amount of money extended by the Fed's liquidity facilities, we subtract the Fed's holdings of Treasuries and MBS from the size of the Fed's total balance sheet. This shows that these facilities rose $926 billion from the last week of February until they peaked at $1.2 trillion during the week of

May 13. They were down to $566 billion by the end of 2020 (*Fig. 6*). On July 28, the Fed announced an extension through December 31 of its lending facilities that were scheduled to expire on or around September 30.[46] On November 30, the Fed extended several of its lending facilities through March 31.[47]

The FOMC statement released at the end of the committee's final meeting of 2020 on December 16 stated that the Fed would "continue to increase its holdings of Treasury securities by at least $80 billion per month and of agency mortgage backed securities by at least $40 billion per month until substantial further progress has been made toward the Committee's maximum employment and price stability goals."[48] That was the first time since the GVC had started that the Fed had specified the likely monthly pace of security purchases.[49] From February through December, the average monthly increases in the Fed's holdings of Treasuries and MBS were $207 billion and $59 billion, respectively.

Pragmatic Pivoter

In my *Fed Watching* book, Chapter 8 is titled "Jerome Powell: The Pragmatic Pivoter." Recall that the S&P 500 plunged 19.8% from September 20 through December 24, 2018 in reaction to an October 3 interview in which Powell suggested that he expected to be raising interest rates in 2019 because "we're a long way from neutral." He added, "We may go past neutral."[50]

The market's adverse reaction caused him to change his mind. During November, he signaled that the Fed might pause hiking interest rates for a while. By early June 2019, he suggested that the next move by the Fed might be to lower interest rates. At the July 31 meeting, the FOMC voted to lower the federal funds rate's target range from 2.25%–2.50% to 2.00%–2.25%, the first rate cut since 2008. In addition, the FOMC decided to terminate quantitative tightening (QT) ahead of schedule. There were two more rate cuts before the end of 2019.

Powell's biggest pivot occurred on March 23, 2020 when he effectively embraced Modern Monetary Theory. As we noted in the Introduction, in his February 26, 2019 congressional testimony on monetary policy, he disparaged MMT, rejecting the idea that the Fed would ever help combat the impact of spiraling fiscal deficits by keeping interest rates low. In his March 3, 2020 unscheduled press conference, which followed the emergency meeting of the FOMC that day, Powell reasserted, "So, in terms of fiscal policy, again, [that's] not our role. We have a full plate with monetary policy. [It's] [n]ot our role to give advice to the fiscal policymakers.[51]

In his March 15 press conference, which followed the unscheduled FOMC emergency meeting that day, Powell still insisted on a clear separation of fiscal and monetary policymaking:

> You know, we have different tools. I think we do, actually, work pretty closely with the Treasury Department . . . and cooperate with them on things, with clear lines of delineation. For example, the Treasury Department has authority over fiscal policy. That's not our job. It's their job, with other parts of the Administration. It's just . . . that for us with monetary policy. We have sole responsibility for monetary policy and strong instructions from Congress to conduct it in an independent, nonpolitical way.

Powell observed, "We've had one round of fiscal policy, [and] another coming. I think fiscal policy is a way to direct relief, really, to particular populations and groups."[52]

What a difference a GVC makes! Now Powell was all for MMT all the time, or at least until an effective vaccine was developed and widely distributed. He also wanted more rounds of fiscal policy support.

In his April 29 press conference, he crossed the line, mentioning the word "fiscal" 11 times. A central theme of his comments was that "[t]his is the time to use the great fiscal power of the United States . . . to do what we can to support the economy and try to get through this with as little damage to the longer-run productive capacity of the economy as possible." He implied that the Fed would do everything possible to enable more fiscal stimulus. That all adds up to MMT.[53]

In a CBS *60 Minutes* interview on Sunday, May 17, Powell said that the outlook for the economy depends on "what happens with the coronavirus." In fact, he didn't expect that the economy could fully recover until there was a vaccine. Nevertheless, he tried to be optimistic, saying, "In the long run, and even in the medium run, you wouldn't want to bet against the American economy. This economy will recover."

He clearly stated that the Fed has lots of firepower left: "Well, there's a lot more we can do. We've done what we can as we go. But I will say that we're not out of ammunition by a long shot. No, there's really no limit to what we can do with these lending programs that we have. So there's a lot more we can do to support the economy, and we're committed to doing everything we can as long as we need to."[54]

In his CBS interview, Powell said, "I continue to think, and my colleagues on the Federal Open Market Committee continue to think, that negative interest rates is probably not an appropriate or useful policy for us here in the United States." He rightly observed that negative rates have existed in the Eurozone and Japan without success, and that they introduce "distortions into the financial system. . . ." The Fed obviously knows something about how to distort the financial markets!

By the way, Powell was asked whether the Fed had responded to the GVC simply by flooding the system with money. Powell candidly stated, "Yes. We did. That's another way to think about it. We did." Then he was asked where the money came from: "Did you just print it?" Again, Powell acknowledged, "We print it digitally. So as a central bank, we have the ability to create money digitally. And we do that by buying Treasury bills or bonds or other government-guaranteed securities. And that actually increases the money supply. We also print actual currency, and we distribute that through the Federal Reserve banks." When asked to compare the Fed's response to the GVC versus the GFC, Powell said:

> So the things we're doing now are substantially larger. The asset purchases that we're doing are a multiple of the programs that were done during the last crisis. And it's very different this time. In the last crisis, the problems were in the financial system. So they were providing support for the banking system. Here, really, the problems are in what we call the real economy, actual companies that make and sell goods and services. And what's happening to them is that many of them are closed or just not having any revenue. And we're trying to do what we can to get them through this period where they're perfectly good companies that have had, you know, sound financial condition as recently as February, but now they have no business. And they have fixed costs. So we're trying to help them get through that period.

On May 29, 2020, at an online event hosted by Princeton University's Griswold Center for Economic Policy Studies, Powell readily acknowledged: "We crossed a lot of red lines that had not been crossed before." He added, "I'm very confident that this is the situation where you do that and then you figure it out."[55]

During his June 10 press conference, in his prepared remarks, Powell said:

> I would stress that [the Fed has] lending powers, not spending powers. The Fed cannot grant money to particular

beneficiaries. . . . Elected officials have the power to tax and spend and to make decisions about where we, as a society, should direct our collective resources. The CARES Act and other legislation provide direct help to people and businesses and communities. This direct support can make a critical difference not just in helping families and businesses in a time of need, but also in limiting long-lasting damage to our economy.[56]

During the Q&A session of his July 29 press conference, Powell responded: "Fiscal policy . . . can address things that we can't address. If there are particular groups that need help, that need direct monetary help—not a loan, but an actual grant as the PPP program showed—you can save a lot of businesses and a lot of jobs with those in a case where lending a company money might not be the right answer. The company might not want to take a loan out in order to pay workers who can't work because there's no business."[57]

In prepared remarks at his September 16 press conference, Powell said: "The path forward will also depend on the policy actions taken across all parts of the government to provide relief and to support the recovery for as long as needed." In the Q&A, he warned that "as the months pass . . . if there isn't additional support and there isn't a job for some of those people who are from industries where it's going to be very hard to find new work, then that will start to show up in economic activity. It will also show up in things like evictions and foreclosures and, you know, things that will scar and damage the economy."[58]

At the National Association for Business Economics' virtual annual meeting on October 6, the Fed chair reiterated his call for more MMT: "By contrast, the risks of overdoing it seem, for now, to be smaller. Even if policy actions ultimately prove to be greater than needed, they will not go to waste. The recovery will be stronger and move faster if monetary policy and fiscal policy continue to work side by side to provide support to the economy until it is clearly out of the woods."[59]

An editorial in the October 7 issue of *The Wall Street Journal* commented: "It's important to understand how unusual this is. The Fed's job is monetary policy and financial regulation. Yet here is a Fed chief lobbying Congress, and the public, on behalf of one side of a fiscal debate."[60]

Don't Fight T-Fed

Powell's call for fiscal policymakers to do more did not fall on deaf ears. Congress did respond quickly and aggressively to the GVC.

On March 6, the Coronavirus Preparedness and Response Supplemental Appropriations Act was enacted. It provided $8.3 billion in supplemental appropriations, designated as emergency funding, for federal agencies to respond to the coronavirus crisis and direct spending to allow for broader use of and payment for telehealth services for Medicare beneficiaries during the emergency period. The lion's share of the increase in the budget authority was allocated to the Labor, Health and Human Services, Education Appropriations Subcommittee, which funds the CDC and related organizations. The Families First Coronavirus Response Act was enacted on March 18. It provided paid sick leave, tax credits, and free Covid-19 testing. It expanded food assistance and unemployment benefits and increased Medicaid funding.

The biggest fiscal response to the GVC during 2020 was President Trump's signing of the CARES Act on March 27. It was the largest economic relief bill in American history. Besides the aforementioned $454 billion to the Treasury for the Fed's purposes, it offered substantial financial relief for consumers, healthcare providers, states, and small business. Altogether, the CARES Act provided total assistance of $2.2 trillion.

In its preliminary estimate of the effects of the Act, dated April 27, the CBO estimated that it would increase federal deficits by about $1.7 trillion over the 2020–30 period. The CBO observed: "Although the act provides financial assistance totaling more than $2 trillion, the projected cost is less than that because some of that assistance is in the form of loan guarantees, which are not estimated to have a net effect on the budget."[61]

A very important component of the CARES Act was the $454 billion the Treasury secretary was authorized to allocate to fund the Fed's various emergency lending facilities. That's because this funding was expected to be leveraged by the Fed at a ratio of almost 10-to-1 into $4 *trillion* in loans for the US economy. Notably, however, this capital would not impact the deficit because the Treasury was expecting eventually to recoup it. It was being provided simply to backstop the Fed's lending activities.

The provisions in the CARES Act with the largest deficit effects were the PPP, the relief check to individual taxpayers, and the expansion of unemployment insurance benefits. They were expected to account for most of the projected increase in outlays from the CARES Act.

Under PPP, CARES allocated $349 billion of loans to small businesses and nonprofits to help them pay employee wages and other costs. All loan payments were deferred for six months, and any part of the loan used over the next eight weeks for payroll, rent, utilities, and mortgage interest would be forgiven in full if employees were retained.

The Act expanded eligibility and number of weeks of benefit for unemployment compensation as well as increased the weekly benefit amount by $600. It provided support payments of $1,200 per qualifying adult and $500 per dependent child. The unemployment insurance and the recovery outlays were expected to amount to $266 billion and $151 billion, respectively.

The Act gave $100 billion to eligible healthcare providers—such as hospitals, long-term care providers, and physicians' practices—to reimburse them for expenses or lost revenues due to Covid-19. Costs could include building temporary facilities, leasing properties, and purchasing supplies, equipment, and tests.

The CARES Act also provided up to $46 billion in loans from the Treasury to certain industries: $25 billion to passenger airlines and related businesses; $4 billion to cargo air carriers; and $17 billion to businesses critical to national security, according to Treasury's guidelines. Cruise lines were ineligible for CARES loans, as borrowers must be created or organized in the US and employ Americans as majority of their workforce.

After quickly concluding that all that was not enough, Congress passed a supplemental $483 billion Covid-19 related economic relief bill on April 24. The Paycheck Protection Program and Health Care Enhancement Act provided additional appropriations for small business loans, healthcare providers, and Covid-19 testing. The appropriation for PPP loans was increased by $321 billion.

Yet another pandemic relief act was passed by Congress at the end of 2020. This one totaled about $900 billion and included another round of support for small businesses and unemployed workers. President Trump initially refused to sign it unless the amount for relief checks sent to eligible taxpayers was raised from $600 to $2,000. He signed off on it on December 27. Those qualifying for the maximum stimulus payment included individuals earning up to $75,000 in adjusted gross income (AGI), married couples filing jointly earning up to $150,000 in AGI, or heads of households earning up to $112,500 in AGI.

The result of all this fiscal stimulus was a dramatic widening of the federal budget deficit. Just prior to the GVC, the CBO projected that it would be $1.1 trillion during fiscal 2020. On April 27, that projection was raised by $1.7 trillion to $2.8 trillion. Sure enough, the 12-month sum of the federal deficit was $3.1 trillion through September, which was the last month of fiscal 2020 (*Fig. 7*). From February through September, this moving-sum of the deficit jumped $2.0 trillion, from $1.1 trillion to $3.1 trillion. Over the same period, the Fed's purchases of US Treasury securities rose $2.1 trillion to a record $2.3 trillion.

The Fed and the Treasury had joined forces in the MMT crusade to drown the virus in liquidity during the week of March 23-27 as a result of QE4ever and the CARES Act. We might as well consolidate the two of them in our minds to "T-Fed." That was the gist of our October 12 *Morning Briefing* titled "Don't Fight T-Fed." We concluded: "T-Fed was born on March 23, the day that the Fed adopted QE4ever. Ever since then, Fed officials have been basically saying: 'More, more, more!' They want another round of MMT. They don't call it that, but that's what they are asking for."[62]

In summary, the Fed's pandemic response was unprecedented. Prior to the GVC, Fed officials were dismissive of MMT since it crossed a line into the realm of fiscal policy. The Fed does monetary policy. Congress and the White House do fiscal policy. Period! Nothing to see here. Move on.

During the GVC, Fed officials broke with tradition by calling on the fiscal authorities to do much more to support the economy. They made it very clear that they would continue to help finance the resulting federal deficits by purchasing most, if not all, of the Treasury debt issued to pay for more fiscal stimulus.

Yield-Curve Targeting

What if another big round of deficit-financed fiscal spending had pushed up bond yields and mortgage rates? That would have been a big setback for MMT crusaders, the Fed among them. The 10-year Treasury bond yield remained below 1.00% since MMT Day (March 23) through the end of 2020.

The Fed did have a way to keep bond yields from soaring: yield-curve targeting (YCT), officially targeting the bond yield. The remarkable stability of the bond yield near record lows during 2020 suggested to us that the Fed might have been capping the bond yield below 1.00% without officially saying so.

Ever since March 23, Powell repeatedly stated that the Fed intended to keep interest rates close to zero for a very long time. At his June 10 press conference, he famously said: "We're not thinking about raising rates. We're not even thinking about thinking about raising rates."[63] He reiterated that policy in his July 29 press conference, saying: "We have held our policy interest rate near zero since mid-March and have stated that we will keep it there until we are confident that the economy has weathered recent events and is on track to achieve our maximum employment and price stability goals."[64]

Remember that the Fed lowered the federal funds rate by 100 basis points to zero on March 15. No target was set for the bond yield at that time or has been since then—so far. At Powell's June 10 press conference, Nick Timiraos of *The Wall Street Journal* asked the Fed chair about the possibility of "yield caps." Powell revealed that at the latest meeting of the FOMC the participants received a briefing on the historical experience with YCT, and he said that they would evaluate it in upcoming meetings. Here is the excerpt on YCT from the June 10 FOMC Minutes:

The second staff briefing reviewed the yield caps or targets (YCT) policies that the Federal Reserve followed during and after World War II and that the Bank of Japan and the Reserve Bank of Australia are currently employing. . . . [T]hese three experiences suggested that credible YCT policies can control government bond yields, pass through to private rates, and, in the absence of exit considerations, may not require large central bank purchases of government debt. But the staff also highlighted the potential for YCT policies to require the central bank to purchase very sizable amounts of government debt under certain circumstances . . . and the possibility that, under YCT policies, monetary policy goals might come in conflict with public debt management goals, which could pose risks to the independence of the central bank.[65]

So how did the Fed keep a lid on the 10-year bond yield during 2020 without formally implementing YCT? Simple: The Fed bought almost all the bonds that the Treasury issued. From February through December 2020, the Treasury issued $443 billion in bonds with maturities exceeding 10 years. Over that same period, the Fed purchased $411 billion of such bonds (*Fig. 8*).

Chapter 3
Allied Bombing Campaign

Lagarde's Turn

Christine Lagarde replaced Mario Draghi as the head of the European Central Bank (ECB) on November 1, 2019. Before starting her new position, she said she hoped she wouldn't have to follow up Draghi's "whatever it takes" monetary policy with more of the same. In fact, on September 12, 2019, before packing up his office, Draghi revived the ECB's Asset Purchase Programme (APP) with an open-ended commitment to purchase €20 billion per month in net assets without setting any termination date, i.e., "APP4ever" as we called it. It was set to take effect on November 1, 2019, the very same day that Lagarde took over the helm of the ECB.

Ironically, Lagarde had her first what-ever-it-takes moment just four months later on March 2. As a result of the pandemic, she said that the bank was ready to take "appropriate and targeted" measures to deal with the economic fallout from the virus." She observed, "The coronavirus outbreak is a fast-developing situation, which creates risks for the economic outlook and the functioning of financial markets."[66]

On March 12, the members of the ECB's Governing Council announced a comprehensive package of monetary policy measures, but disappointed markets when they did not cut interest rates. Nevertheless, the bank remained committed to maintaining historically low interest rates on the main refinancing operations, the marginal lending facility, and the deposit facility at 0.00%, 0.25%, and -0.50%, respectively.[67]

The ECB eased conditions on bank lending to small and medium-sized businesses (SMEs), or "those affected most by the spread of the coronavirus," stated the March 12 press release on the decision. Since 2014, the ECB has used Targeted Longer-Term Refinancing Operations (TLTRO) to encourage bank lending. Key parameters of the third series of this stimulus (TLTRO III, initiated in 2019) were modified to support the continued access of firms and households to bank credit in the face of disruptions and temporary funding shortages associated with the coronavirus outbreak. The changes would apply to all TLTRO III operations. Substantially lower rates were granted to banks to lend to SMEs, with more favorable terms offered from June 2020 to June 2021 for the ECB's TLTRO III.[68] Lagarde said during her post-meeting press conference that the ECB felt this would more effectively support the financial system than would broadly lowering interest rates.

Lagarde repeatedly declared that Eurozone governments should help support the global economy during the pandemic, asserting that central banks can't carry the onus alone. At her March 12 press conference, she said that all policy institutions are "called upon to take timely and targeted actions to address the public health challenge of containing the spread of the coronavirus and mitigate the economic impact." She added, "In particular, an ambitious and coordinated fiscal policy response is required to support businesses and workers at risk." Lagarde expressed disappointment that the Eurozone's fiscal efforts as of her press conference amounted to less than 1.0% of GDP.

Referring once again to her predecessor Mario Draghi, Lagarde added: "I don't have a claim to history for being whatever-it-takes number two. I really would like all of us to join forces, and I very much hope that the fiscal authorities will appreciate that we will only deal with the shock if we come together."[69] That statement was just six days before Lagarde assumed the whatever-it-takes mantle she had hoped to avoid.

The ECB joined the allied shock-and-awe bombing campaign on March 18 with its Pandemic Emergency Purchase Programme (PEPP), committing to buy €750 billion of private- and public-sector Eurozone securities. The press release stated, "Purchases will be conducted until the end of 2020 and will include all the asset categories eligible under the existing asset purchase programme (APP)." In addition, the ECB expanded the range of eligible assets under its Corporate Sector Purchase Programme (CSPP) to non-financial commercial paper, making all commercial paper of sufficient credit quality eligible for purchase under CSPP.[70]

At the June 4 meeting of the Governing Council, the ECB upped the PEPP ante by €600 billion to a total of €1,350 billion. The policy statement noted: "[P]urchases will continue to be conducted in a flexible manner over time, across asset classes and among jurisdictions." No firm end date was set for the purchases, which were to be extended at least through the end of June 2021 but which wouldn't end until the bank "judges that the coronavirus crisis phase is over." Proceeds from maturing securities would be reinvested at least until the end of 2022.

The PEPP's "temporary" net asset purchases of €120 billion per month would continue for at least the rest of the year. Under the APP, monthly net asset purchases of €20 billion would "run for as long as necessary to reinforce the accommodative impact of its policy rates, and to end shortly before it starts raising the key ECB interest rates." The ECB's key interest rates remained unchanged. Interest rates were expected to remain "at their present or lower levels" until inflation moved "consistently" toward the ECB's 2.0% inflation goal.[71]

Following the bank's April 30 monetary policy meeting, the ECB decided to conduct a new series of seven additional longer-term refinancing operations called "pandemic emergency longer-term refinancing operations" (PELTROs) to provide liquidity to the euro area financial system and to preserve the smooth functioning of money markets by providing a backstop to the March "longer-term refinancing operations" (LTROs).[72]

As the ECB provided more aid, it also lowered the standards on the credit quality of assets eligible for purchase and expanded the types. No doubt, the expansion of eligible credit instruments was necessary to prevent the ECB from owning a higher market share of previously eligible instruments than would be desirable.

On Thursday, December 10, the ECB announced that it would inject the Eurozone economy with more doses of liquidity, warning that the economic crisis caused by the pandemic was likely to linger well into 2022 despite the rollout of new vaccines. The ECB's December 10 press release announced PEPP-for-longer. The Governing Council decided "to increase the envelope" of the PEPP by €500 billion to a total of €1,850 billion. It also extended the horizon for net purchases under the PEPP to at least the end of March 2022. The ECB declared, "In any case, the Governing Council will conduct net purchases until it judges that the coronavirus crisis phase is over."

The TLTRO III conditions were recalibrated. The period over which considerably more favorable terms would apply was extended by 12 months to June 2022. Three additional operations would also be conducted between June and December 2021.[73]

The ECB's balance sheet rose €2.3 trillion from the end of February to a record €7.0 trillion during the last week of 2020 (*Fig. 9*). Over this same period, securities held for monetary policy purposes increased €1.0 trillion to a record €3.7 trillion, while LTROs jumped €1.2 trillion to a record €1.8 trillion (*Fig. 10*).

All that liquidity couldn't stop the plunge in economic activity as Eurozone governments imposed lockdowns to enforce social distancing. The liquidity was expected to speed the recovery as lockdown restrictions were lifted during the summer. However, another wave of the pandemic during the fall of 2020 resulted in another round of social-distancing restrictions. Meanwhile, as in the US, all the liquidity provided by the ECB averted a widespread credit crunch and boosted asset prices.

At the end of 2020, 10-year government bond yields were at or near record lows in Germany (-0.58%), France (-0.34%), Spain (0.06%), and Italy (0.52%) (*Fig. 11*). The yield spreads between both Italian and Spanish 10-year government bonds and the comparable German bund widened sharply during March but narrowed to near record lows of 110 basis points and 64 basis points by the end of 2020 (*Fig. 12*). Since March 23, the EMU MSCI stock price index (in euros) rose 45.4% by the end of 2020.

The Eurozone's purchasing managers' indexes (PMI) for manufacturing and nonmanufacturing industries bottomed at record lows of 33.4 and 12.0 during April (*Fig. 13*). They rebounded sharply over the next few months. However, while the manufacturing PMI ended 2020 at 55.2, the nonmanufacturing PMI peaked at 54.7 during July and was back down to 46.4 during December 2020 as a result of renewed lockdown restrictions.

The Eurozone Economic Sentiment Indicator, which is highly correlated with the year-over-year growth rate of the region's real GDP, bottomed at 64.9 during April, which was the lowest in the history of the series going back to 1985 (*Fig. 14*). It was up to 90.4 by the end of 2020, still well below the year's high of 103.4 during February.

Lagarde's wish for more fiscal support came true on April 9, when European Union (EU) finance ministers agreed on a new pandemic stimulus package worth €540 billion. However, they couldn't agree on a crucial decision: whether to issue joint debt instruments, called "corona bonds," that would combine debt securities from the 19 Eurozone countries. Germany and the Netherlands, traditionally more fiscally conservative than Italy and Spain, were holdouts.

April's emergency fiscal package targeted workers, businesses, and member states. To support workers, the EU introduced the temporary Support to Mitigate Unemployment Risks in an Emergency initiative. The program made €100 billion of temporary EU loans available to fund countries' employment furlough programs.

In many European countries, companies are encouraged to furlough employees instead of firing them. Furloughed employees are paid some percentage of their prior salary by their employers. In return, they work reduced hours or don't work but remain available to return to the company when better times arrive. The employers are reimbursed for their furlough payments by the government. The programs do not cover those who work off the books. As the pandemic dragged on in 2020, countries extended the duration of their furlough benefits.

Without the furlough programs, unemployment rates would have been much higher in Europe. In the Eurozone, in 2020 the jobless rate rose from 7.3% during January to a high of 8.7% during July. In the US, this rate rose from 3.5% in January to a peak of 14.8% during April. The Eurozone unemployment rate edged down to 8.3% during November and December. In the US, it fell to 6.7% during December 2020.

On July 21, the EU's finance ministers reached agreement on a new bold initiative that was called the "Next Generation EU" (NGEU) fund. It authorized the European Commission (EC), the executive arm of the EU, to create a €750 billion recovery fund, which would be distributed among the countries and sectors most impacted by the Covid-19 pandemic and would take the form of grants and loans. The EU has historically avoided issuing bonds and only had about €50 billion of debt outstanding at the time. Member nations historically have funded themselves independently. But this deal recognized that the poorer nations needed funding from their wealthier counterparts—without which the EU possibly could splinter apart. The pandemic recovery fund was authorized to make €390 billion of grants to economically weak EU members, with the rest of the funding made available through loans.

The new deal meant that the EU would become a major borrower in global financial markets for the first time. It plans to repay the money by 2058. The EC intended to propose new taxes on financial transactions and fines on greenhouse gases released by companies. Technology companies could also expect a "digital levy."

In a July 23 ECB blog post, Lagarde strongly endorsed the NGEU. She wrote that she hoped to "forge a new Europe out of this crisis."[74] At the ECB's September 10 monetary policy meeting, the Governing Council decided to maintain its extraordinarily accommodative policy despite signs of recovery. An analysis in the ECB's September 24 *Economic Bulletin* promoted the NGEU. It emphasized that the "monetary and fiscal policies, although implemented independently in the euro area, are currently acting in a mutually reinforcing way."[75]

Indeed, the precedent-setting NGEU represents no less than a new fiscal union of European nations, borne of the Covid-19 crisis. The *Economic Bulletin* states:

> NGEU constitutes a new and innovative element of the European fiscal framework. It will result in the issuance of sizeable supranational debt over the coming years, and its establishment has [signaled] a political readiness to design a common fiscal tool when the need arises. This innovation, while a one-off, could also imply lessons for Economic and

Monetary Union, which still lacks a permanent fiscal capacity at supranational level for macroeconomic [stabilization] in deep crises.

Speaking in an interview ahead of *The Wall Street Journal's* CEO Council on October 6, Lagarde said that the ECB was prepared to add more stimulus to support the "shaky" European recovery. "We are not the only game in town anymore," she added, indicating her appreciation for the recent government actions to provide stimulus.[76]

By the way, perhaps the new fund should have been called the "New Green EU." An interesting component of the NGEU is its commitment to fund climate-friendly technologies. Lagarde noted in her July 23 blog post that 30% of spending in both the NGEU fund and the EU budget "will have to be linked to the climate transition and all spending should be consistent with the Paris climate goals." She explained, "This means that more than €500 billion will be spent on greening the European economy over the coming years—the biggest green stimulus of all time." She concluded, "Countries will only be able to receive money if they submit recovery and resilience plans that contribute to the green and digital transitions."

BOJ on Faster Track

In response to the WHO's pandemic declaration on March 11, the Bank of Japan's Policy Board met in an emergency session on March 16.

Like the ECB, the Bank of Japan (BOJ) resisted lowering its key short-term rate further into negative territory from -0.10%. It also maintained its zero percent target for 10-year Japanese government bond yields, according to the bank's statement. The central bank did, however, significantly increase the supply of funds and added generous support to the equity markets. The BOJ raised its total target for corporate bond holdings and commercial paper by ¥1 trillion ($9 billion) each, to ¥4.2 trillion ($39 billion) and ¥3.2 trillion ($30 billion). It also pledged to double the annual pace at which it would purchase equity ETFs and J-REITs (Japanese real estate investment trusts) to around ¥12 trillion ($115 billion) and ¥180 billion ($1.7 billion). The incremental purchases were set to continue until September. Additionally, the BOJ created a new loan program that extended one-year, interest-free loans to financial institutions.[77]

The BOJ's March easing was intended to address the immediate market distress, so more was expected to come when the bank's policy committee met next on April 27–28; BOJ Governor Haruhiko Kuroda said as much after the March meeting.

On April 7, the Japanese government unveiled a record ¥108.2 trillion ($1.0 trillion) stimulus package to offset the economic damage as Prime Minister Shinzo Abe declared a state of emergency. The country's export markets were paralyzed, the summer Olympics were postponed, and the country's major cities now faced the prospect of extended stay-at-home orders. The stimulus package included subsidies for firms that kept workers on the payroll. The plan also called for ¥4 trillion ($37 billion) in cash payments to struggling households and another ¥2.3 trillion ($21 billion) for small businesses.[78]

At its April 27 policy meeting, the BOJ pledged to buy an unlimited amount of government bonds to keep borrowing costs low as the government tried to spend its way out of the growing economic pain from the Covid-19 pandemic. To ease corporate funding strains, the BOJ said it would boost by threefold the maximum amount of corporate bonds and commercial paper it buys to ¥20 trillion ($186 billion).[79]

Also, in late May, Japanese Prime Minister Shinzo Abe's cabinet approved another ¥118 trillion ($1.1 trillion) stimulus package. The new package raised Japan's total spending to combat the virus fallout to ¥234 trillion ($2.2 trillion), or about 40% of GDP. That ranked among the world's largest fiscal support packages to deal with the pandemic.

To fund the costs, Japan issued an additional ¥31.9 trillion in government bonds under the second supplementary budget for the fiscal year ending in March 2021. That pushed new bond issuance for that fiscal year to a record ¥90 trillion ($833 billion). The BOJ was expected to keep borrowing costs low with its Yield Curve Control policy targeting the bank's short-term interest rate at -0.10% and the 10-year bond yield at around zero.[80]

On July 21, Finance Minister Taro Aso said that the Japanese government's budget wouldn't set a spending cap on requests aimed at fighting the Covid-19 pandemic for the fiscal year that began in April 2021. The budget ceiling is usually set around midyear by the Finance Ministry to keep tabs on spending requests from ministries for next year's budget, to be compiled in December.

The government would ask ministries to keep requests for other spending in line with the current fiscal year's initial budget totaling a record ¥102.7 trillion ($951 billion), Aso said at a cabinet meeting. The government then would set aside an unspecified amount of budget requests to respond to "urgently needed expenses" to battle the fallout from the pandemic.[81]

On August 28, Shinzo Abe, the longest-serving Japanese prime minister in history, resigned, citing health reasons. Soon after he was elected to a second term in 2012, he launched an ambitious package of policies popularly known as "Abenomics." The policy program included three so-called arrows—massive monetary stimulus, increased government spending, and structural reforms. On September 16, BOJ Governor Haruhiko Kuroda pledged to work closely with the country's new Prime Minister Yoshihide Suga to support the economy in keeping with Abenomics.

The BOJ's balance sheet soared by ¥118 trillion ($1.1 trillion) from the last week of February through 2020's final week to a record high of ¥703 trillion ($6.5 trillion) (*Fig. 15*). The BOJ's balance sheet had been expanding ever since it implemented its program of Quantitative and Qualitative Easing (QQE) on April 4, 2013. Since March 16, 2020, the QQE treadmill's speed setting had been increased considerably.

By one measure, Japan has experienced a V-shaped recovery from the depths of the pandemic. The manufacturing PMI plunged from 48.8 at the start of 2020 to a record low of 38.4 during May. It was back up to the breakeven point of 50.0 by December 2020 (*Fig. 16*).

All Together Now

Why did Forrest Gump, the fictional character in the movie about his life, run so much? Our theory is that running was the way that Forrest dealt with adversity. It must have been exhilarating to hear people cheer him on as he jogged by chanting: "Run, Forrest, run!"

Since the GFC, central bankers have been committed to minimizing our adversities by running their ultra-easy monetary policies longer and faster. They told us that they would eventually stop doing so when it was time to normalize. That seemed possible around 2018. But by 2019, the central bankers were convinced that it was too soon to stop running. Since the GVC of 2020, their rallying cry has been "Run, Forrest, run!"

Since the last week of February 2020 through the end of that virus-infected year, the combined assets (in US dollars) on the balance sheets of the Fed, the ECB, and the BOJ soared 56%, or $8.1 trillion, to a record $22.6 trillion (*Fig. 17*). Here are the increases over those same periods along with their end-of-year record highs for the three central banks: the Fed ($3.2 trillion to $7.3 trillion), the ECB ($3.4 trillion to $8.5 trillion), and the BOJ ($1.5 trillion, to $6.8 trillion) (*Fig. 18*).

Run, Forrest, run!

Chapter 4
World War V

Three Fronts

In many ways, the GVC of 2020 was a world war against the virus (WWV). Wars often have more than one front. When WWV broke out in early 2020, it immediately occurred along three fronts. The conflict started on the health front but rapidly spread to the financial and economic fronts. Initially, the pandemic of fear spread through global financial markets as fast as the viral pandemic. But the rapid shock-and-awe counterattacks mounted by Fed officials and their overseas allies quickly saved the day. Lost ground was quickly reclaimed so that by the end of 2020, the most progress had been made on the financial front.

On the economic front, the US economy was in full retreat during March and April. But by the late spring and early summer, it rebounded much faster and better than had been widely expected. However, eventual victors normally experience lots of setbacks in their efforts to defeat their enemies. During WWV, a third wave of the pandemic in the final months of 2020 resulted in another round of social-distancing restrictions that started to weigh on the economic recovery.

The most important front, of course, was the health front. By the end of 2020, the remarkably fast development of vaccines—i.e., weapons of mass destruction against the virus—suggested that WWV might be won by the second half of 2021 if enough people were inoculated against the disease by then. However, there were still plenty of setbacks around the world as the virus continued to spread in many countries. The war will be over once victory has been achieved on the health front.

There was nothing the Fed could do on the health front. The Fed's rapid response to the GVC was to flood the financial system with liquidity. The goal was to offset the negative financial and economic consequences of the pandemic with ultra-easy monetary policy. Fed officials frequently stated that they would continue to fight the good fight on the financial and economic fronts until a vaccine had resulted in victory on the health front.

To a large extent, the GFC of 2008 was a typical business-cycle downturn. It was preceded by an economic boom that was led by speculative excesses, particularly in the housing industry. When that bubble burst, a credit crunch worsened the resulting recession, with real GDP falling 4.0% from the fourth quarter of 2007 through the second quarter of 2009. The NBER's Dating Committee ruled that it lasted 18 months, from December 2007 through June 2009.

The declaration on March 11, 2020 of a pandemic by the WHO precipitated the GVC as governments around the world locked down their economies to slow the spread of the virus. The result was a severe global recession. However, the GVC was unique. In many ways, it could be viewed not only as a world war but also as a major natural disaster that hit the entire global economy. Initially, it did trigger a credit crunch. But the world's major central banks quickly halted the credit crunch by pouring lots of liquidity into global financial markets.

Financial Front

Perhaps the best way to gauge the dramatic turn of events on the financial front during the first few months of 2020 is to review the ups and downs of the credit-quality yield spread between the high-yield corporate bond composite and the 10-year US Treasury bond. It fell to near historical lows at the end of 2019 through January 2020. It was 392 basis points at the end of January (*Fig. 19*). Investors were still clearly reaching for yield as a result of the Fed's three cuts in the federal funds rate during the second half of 2019.

The pandemic of fear unleashed by the viral pandemic caused the yield spread to widen dramatically during February and March to a high of 1,062 basis points on March 23. Investors were no longer reaching for yield. Instead, they joined an unprecedented mad dash for cash, as evidenced by massive outflows out of bond funds and into liquid assets, including money market funds and bank deposits, especially during March (*Fig. 20* and *Fig. 21*). Business borrowers dashed to draw down their lines of credit at the banks (*Fig. 22*).

The S&P 500 plunged 33.9% from February 19 through March 23 (*Fig. 23*). That all happened in 23 trading days. The S&P 500 VIX, which is a measure of stock market volatility, soared from 12.1 on January 21 to peak at 82.7 on March 16 (*Fig. 24*). That slightly exceeded the peak of the GFC. While individual investors were bailing out of bonds and stocks, our institutional accounts told us during Zoom conference calls that they wanted to rebalance out of bonds and into stocks. But they couldn't do so because the bond market had turned so illiquid. It was impossible to find bond buyers at other than fire-sale prices.

That all changed in a heartbeat on March 23 when the Fed announced QE4ever. In our March 25 *Morning Briefing*, we concluded that the Fed had just made the low for the stock market. Credit-quality yield spreads also peaked immediately after the Fed's announcement. Literally overnight, the mad dash for cash was transformed into a mad dash for stocks. In the bond market, the reach-for-yield trade was back as the credit-quality spread between high-yield bonds and the 10-year Treasury bond narrowed dramatically. It was back down to its pre-pandemic range at the beginning of the year by November.

The 10-year US Treasury bond yield fell to a record low of 0.52% on August 4 (*Fig. 25*). It then trended higher toward 1.00% over the rest of the year but remained below that level. We observed that since March 23, the Fed had been buying US Treasury notes and bonds almost as fast as the Treasury was issuing them to fund the rapidly widening federal budget deficit, suggesting that the Fed had implemented a de facto policy of YCT.

Just as impressive was that both investment-grade and non-investment-grade corporate bond yields fell to record lows during the last three days of 2020 (*Fig. 26*). The Fed's March 23 announcement that, in addition to QE4ever, the central bank would backstop the corporate bond market—including even BBB-rated investment-grade bonds that had been downgraded to junk by the credit-rating agencies—quickly ended the credit crunch. As it turned out, the Fed's actual purchases of corporate bonds was insignificant because the financial markets had started to function again; there was no longer any need.

The credit crunch was over as quickly as it had started thanks to the Fed's actual and promised intervention in the credit markets. Indeed, issuance of nonfinancial corporate bonds rose to a record $1.5 trillion over the 12 months through November, with most of that borrowing occurring following the Fed's March 23 announcement (*Fig. 27*). Some of those proceeds were used to pay down credit lines at the banks and bolster corporate liquidity. Some refinanced debt. And some seem to have financed a remarkable rebound in capital spending.

While all this was going on, the stock market received most of the attention in the financial press. Many investment strategists predicted that the S&P 500 would retest its March 23 low after its initial dramatic rebound. We didn't agree given our insights into the pent-up demand for stocks we perceived as institutional investors were rebalancing their portfolios out of bonds and into stocks. The S&P 500 never looked back. Instead, it rose above the February 19 high of 3386.15 on August 18. By the end of 2020, it closed at 3756.07, up 67.9% since March 23 and up 16.3% for the year.

Economic Front

The GVC started in China and spread to the rest of the world from there. China's economy was the first in the world to be hit hard by the pandemic. It was also the first to recover from the pandemic. To contain the virus outbreak, the Chinese government responded with extreme social-distancing measures, including strict lockdowns, which immediately had extremely adverse effects on China's economy. The severity of the economic damage was first demonstrated with the release of February's PMIs in early March. They were in unprecedented freefalls. The official manufacturing PMI plunged to 35.7 in February from 50.0 during January. February's official nonmanufacturing PMI collapsed to 29.6 from 54.1 the month before (*Fig. 28*).

Other monthly indicators confirmed the damage done to China's economy by the lockdowns. On a year-over-year basis, industrial production growth dropped from 6.8% during December to a low of -13.5% during January and February. Inflation-adjusted retail sales growth, on a comparable basis, fell from 3.5% to -12.2% over the same period (*Fig. 29*). When real GDP was tabulated and reported for the first quarter, it showed a calamitous decline of 6.8% on a year-over-year basis. By our calculations, that meant that real GDP growth had collapsed 43.0% (saar) during the first quarter (*Fig. 30*).

The lockdown restrictions were gradually eased during March. The result was a remarkably swift economic snapback. The manufacturing and nonmanufacturing PMIs bottomed at 35.7 and 29.6 during February and rebounded back over 50.0 for both during March to 52.0 and 52.3, respectively. Real GDP rose 49.5% and 12.8% (saar) during the second and third quarters.

Might the US and other major economies around the world follow a similar pattern, with the imposition of lockdowns depressing their economies and the easing of lockdowns resulting in a swift rebound in economic activity?

The US economy turned catatonic when state governors issued stay-in-place orders during late March. In the US, the first sign of trouble in the economic data was in March's IHS Markit flash estimate for the US nonmanufacturing PMI, released in late March. It fell from 53.4 during January and 49.4 during February to 39.1 during March. The PMIs reported by the Institute for Supply Management (ISM) in early April showed the manufacturing index down from 50.1 in February to 49.1 in March and the nonmanufacturing index down from 57.3 to 52.5 over the same period (*Fig. 31*).

In early April, the Bureau of Labor Statistics reported that March payroll employment fell 701,000, while the number of unemployed jumped 1.4 million.

On April 29, the Bureau of Economic Analysis reported that real GDP dropped 4.8% (saar) during the first quarter. It was a preliminary estimate and was subsequently revised to show a 5.0% decline. The NBER's Dating Committee announced that the economy had peaked during February and entered a recession during March. It was obvious that the worst was yet to come, since the lockdowns started in late March—the final month of the first quarter—and hit the economy much harder during April, the first month of the second quarter.

Sure enough, in early May we learned that the ISM manufacturing and nonmanufacturing PMIs for April dropped to 41.5 and 41.8. April's employment report showed a sickening 20.5 million drop in payroll employment, which counts the number of jobs. The number was subsequently revised to a 22.5 million freefall. The household measure of employment, which counts the number of people with either part-time or full-time jobs, fell 22.2 million during April, with the number of unemployed workers jumping by 15.9 million and the labor force falling by 6.2 million. The unemployment rate rose to 14.8% during April, which turned out to be the peak for the year. The distressing employment numbers set the somber tone for subsequent economic indicators released for April. Retail sales plunged 22% from February through April.

The Atlanta Fed's GDPNow tracking model on Friday, May 15 projected a staggering 42.8% decline in real GDP during the second quarter, a downward revision of the 34.9% drop estimated the week before. Inflation-adjusted consumer spending and capital spending were projected to be down 43.6% and 69.4%, respectively.

The Weekly Economic Index (WEI), compiled by the Federal Reserve Bank of New York, showed a year-over-year drop of 11.1% during the week of May 9. The WEI is composed of 10 high-frequency indicators. The Redbook same-store retail sales index and the Rasmussen Consumer Index are used to measure consumer behavior. Also included are initial and continuing unemployment insurance claims, the American Staffing Association Index of temporary and contract employment, and federal tax withholding data. The production indicators include US steel production, electricity output, a measure of fuel sales, and total railroad traffic.

The WEI is scaled to the four-quarter GDP growth rate; for example, if the WEI reads 2% and the current level of the WEI persists for an entire quarter, GDP that quarter should be up 2% year over year. We calculated that if the second quarter's real GDP stayed down 11.1% on a year-over-year basis, it would imply a -37.1% drop (saar) during the quarter.

On Friday, April 24, the CBO released a preliminary economic damage assessment in a blog post. The report projected that real GDP would fall by 40% (saar) during the second quarter and that the unemployment rate would average around 14% for that quarter. For fiscal-year 2020, which ended September, the federal deficit was projected to be $3.7 trillion, with federal debt likely to be 101% of GDP by the end of the fiscal year.[82]

In the May 18 *Morning Briefing* titled "Awakenings," we wrote: "The good news is that the projected growth rate for Q2 is so bad that the depression-like recession might last just two quarters (Q1 and Q2), with real GDP growing again during Q3 and Q4. We are revising our real GDP forecast to a drop of 40% during Q2 followed by gains of 20% during Q3 and 5% during Q4. We no longer expect Q3 to be a down quarter."[83]

On July 30, the second quarter's preliminary GDP report showed a 32.9% (saar) plunge. This was shockingly bad, but not surprisingly so given the lockdowns' abrupt halting of the activity of numerous key industries, particularly many service-producing ones.

State governors started gradually lifting stay-in-place restrictions and opening their economies during May. There were mounting signs that the US economy had experienced an unprecedented two-month recession during March and April, as most of the major monthly economic indicators started to recover during May. Survey data showed that Americans believed that the economy and labor market would improve in coming months. In other words, they didn't expect a long-lasting downturn, let alone a depression.

As the US slowly awakened from this Covid-19 nightmare during the spring of 2020, businesses reopened, and employment started to rebound. We expected that US consumers would spend when stores reopened. May's payroll employment jumped 2.7 million, while the number of unemployed fell 2.1 million. May's retail sales soared 18.3% month over month after dropping 8.2% and 14.7% during March and April (*Fig. 32*).

We have often observed that when American consumers are happy, we spend money and that when we are depressed, we spend even more money, because shopping releases dopamine in our brains, which makes us feel good. Obviously, the GVC wrote a new chapter in the history of consumer behavior. In the May 21 *Morning Briefing*, we wrote: "We aren't virologists, but one widespread side-effect of the virus is evident: Most of us are suffering from cabin fever, which can be depressing. But this time, we haven't been able to seek relief through shopping much because the stores have been closed."[84]

We tried to provide some relief to all of us suffering from cabin fever by compiling a collection of links to YouTube videos with Covid-19-themed parodies of popular songs. We posted it in an April 27 LinkedIn article titled "Cabin Fever Sing Along."[85]

There is a theory that online shopping is even more exciting than shopping in person. You get a double dopamine rush from ordering an item and then opening it upon arrival. During March, online shopping jumped to a record $783.5 billion (saar), accounting for a record 40.0% of GAFO sales.[86] It rose to yet another record high of 50.7% during April (*Fig. 33*).

On its website, the Bureau of Economic Analysis (BEA) explained that the CARES Act provided $300 billion in direct support payments to individuals, distributed mostly in April 2020. The Treasury sent $1,200 to individuals ($2,400 for joint taxpayers) who met specified criteria. In addition, qualified taxpayers with children received $500 for each child.[87] In the BEA's National Income and Product Accounts, these payments to individuals are recorded as "federal social benefit payments to persons," which are included in personal income.

So now we know what happens when the government shuts down the economy—so that we can't go shopping at the malls—while sending support payments. In personal income at annual rates, wages and salaries dropped by $740 billion and proprietors' income fell by $198 billion. Also at annual rates, the $3 trillion jump in social benefits during April more than offset the $1.0 trillion fall in personal income excluding those benefits.

The result was that personal saving (at an annual rate) soared by $4.0 trillion during April as consumption plunged $1.9 trillion, while disposable income was boosted $2.1 trillion by government social benefits (*Fig. 34*). The personal saving rate vaulted from 8.2% during February to 12.7% during March to 33.0% during April! These were all unprecedented moves.

We concluded that a consumer-led V-shaped recovery in coming months was almost inevitable if the reopening of the economy continued without any major setbacks. Sure enough, as the lockdown restrictions were eased, Americans rapidly found cures for their cabin fever, not only by leaving their cabins to shop in brick-and-mortar stores and dine at restaurants but also by purchasing bigger cabins in the suburbs.

Retail sales rose to a new record high during September. Leading the way was housing-related spending, as consumers had decided that it was time to remodel their cabins if they were going to spend more time working, learning, and entertaining at home. They also rushed to buy more new and existing homes in suburban and rural areas in a broad-based wave of de-urbanization triggered by the pandemic. In addition, the pandemic may have convinced many Millennials (who were 24 to 39 years old in 2020) that it was time to buy a house in the suburbs rather than to rent an apartment in cities. The Fed certainly contributed to the resulting housing-related boom by keeping mortgage rates at record-low levels during 2020.

The sum of new plus existing home sales plunged 27% from March through May, and then soared 66% through October to 7.1 million units (saar), the highest since March 2006 (*Fig. 35*). These phenomena have been downright breathtaking to watch. Existing home sales don't directly impact GDP, but they do drive housing-related retail sales.

The result was a consumer-led V-shaped rebound in real GDP. It soared 33.4% (saar) during the third quarter following the 31.4% drop during the second quarter (*Fig. 36*). As of December 23, the Atlanta Fed's GDPNow model was tracking real GDP at a growth rate of 10.4% (saar) during the fourth quarter. Nevertheless, during December, payroll employment was still 9.8 million below its record high during February, and the number of unemployed stood at 10.7 million. The unemployment rate had dropped from a peak of 14.8% during April to 6.7% during December. However, it would have been higher but for the decline in the labor force during the pandemic. Many of the dropouts were parents who had to stay home with their children when their schools offered only online classes.

Health Front

Setbacks on the health front started to weigh on the US economy during the final two months of 2020. The third wave of the pandemic was underway, and it was much worse than the first two waves. Once again, lockdown restrictions were imposed by state governors, though not to the extent as during the first wave.

Despite the setback, the future was looking brighter on the health front. During November, two vaccines had passed their Phase 3 trials with flying colors. Both were deemed to be more than 90% effective. The Food and Drug Administration (FDA) gave them both emergency use authorization, and distribution and inoculations started in December.

Normally, it takes years to formulate a new vaccine, move it through trials, get it approved, and distribute it through the healthcare system. But a number of companies were working on ways to make new vaccines in a matter of months using revolutionary new biotechnologies to speed up the development process. The difference means doctors could inoculate individuals with the vaccine while an outbreak is ongoing rather than years after it has passed. Larger quantities of vaccines can also be made using the new method.

The traditional method of making a vaccine involved killing or weakening a virus and injecting it into the body. Proteins in the virus trigger the body's cells to produce antigens. The new version of developing a vaccine uses genetic sequencing.

On January 10, Chinese scientists uploaded the genetic sequence of the Covid-19 virus to a public website for the scientific community. It took Moderna, a biotech drug company, less than two months to use that genetic sequence to develop a vaccine for Covid-19. Moderna shipped the vaccine out for human testing, putting it in the lead in the race to develop a vaccine. At the time, everyone thought it would take 12 to 18 months to get regulatory approval in the US, but the vaccine was approved just before the year ended thanks to the fast-tracking of development and emergency use authorization.

Messenger RNA (mRNA) is a small molecule that instructs our cells to make proteins. Moderna has used Covid-19's genetic code to create an mRNA that will instruct our cells to make a small amount of Covid-19 proteins. These proteins trigger the production of Covid-19-specific antibodies that provide immunity to the virus. Since the mRNA never goes into the nucleus of cells, there's no concern about its changing the cell's genome.

On Monday, May 18, Moderna announced positive early "Phase 1" findings: Forty-five patients between the ages of 18 and 55 were dosed with 25, 100, or 250 micrograms of the company's experimental vaccine. After receiving a second booster shot, those at the 25 and 100 dosage levels were found with antibody levels that were equal to or exceeded those found in patients who recovered from Covid-19. The press release stated:

> The potential advantages of an mRNA approach to prophylactic vaccines include the ability to combine multiple mRNAs into a single vaccine, rapid discovery to respond to emerging pandemic threats and manufacturing agility derived from the platform nature of mRNA vaccine design and production. Moderna has built a fully integrated manufacturing plant which enables the promise of the technology platform.[88]

So Moderna's vaccine had just passed the Phase 1 clinical trial. There were still Phases 2 and 3 to go. A successful clinical trial process continues until the developer files a marketing application with the US FDA or a regulatory agency in another country for the medication to be approved for doctors to prescribe to patients. (See Appendix 4: The Phases of Clinical Trials.)

By late May, the first wave of the pandemic in the US crested, resulting in the gradual lifting of lockdown restrictions (*Fig. 37* and *Fig. 38*). We had assumed that the vast majority of Americans would respond to the reopening with abundant caution—that is, by keeping their distance from one another and especially by wearing masks in public. They didn't do so. News reports over the long Memorial Day weekend suggested that too many people were throwing caution—and their virus—to the wind, risking undoing the progress made in "flattening the curve," i.e., reducing the infection and hospitalization rates through social distancing. Sure enough, there was a second wave of infections during the early summer. That was followed by a third wave during the final three months of 2020.

Stock prices rallied dramatically during November on news that vaccines were almost ready for distribution. The rally received booster shots on three "vaccine Mondays." On Monday, November 9, Pfizer announced that it had a Covid-19 vaccine ready to go. It was developed with BioNTech using the mRNA technology, but it required extremely cold storage. A week later, on Monday, November 16, Moderna announced that its vaccine required normal refrigeration. Both have remarkable effectiveness rates of over 90%. On Monday, November 23, Oxford-AstraZeneca also reported having a vaccine set to go, but the spotty disclosure of its data reduced the likelihood that it would be fast-tracked by the FDA.

The year 2020 was certainly an *annus horribilis* as a result of WWV. The war was still fierce on the health front by the end of that year. But people were starting to get vaccinated. Unsettling reports that the virus was mutating into a version that spread even more rapidly were countered by assurances from several virologists that the new vaccines should work against variants of the Covid-19 virus much the way the flu vaccines are tweaked every year to protect us from the mostly likely seasonal strain of the flu. We hoped they would be right and that the plague would become merely a pest by the end of 2021.

Chapter 5
Inflation Mandate

Meet FAITH

Prior to the GVC, the Fed embarked on a year-long strategic review of monetary policy largely to address the challenges in achieving its two key congressional mandates: maximum employment and stable prices. The review yielded a revised framework that seemed like an incremental and unremarkable change in Fed policymaking. Fed Chair Jerome Powell discussed the new framework in a rather unremarkable speech on Thursday, August 27, at the annual Jackson Hole economic policy symposium sponsored by the Federal Reserve Bank of Kansas City.[89] He announced that the Fed had amended its inflation-targeting goal from hitting a specific number in favor of average inflation targeting, a.k.a. AIT.

Leading up to the pandemic, it was widely believed that full employment, or close to it, had been achieved. However, the Fed failed to consistently boost inflation up to its 2.0% annual inflation target, which was first set in the FOMC's January 25, 2012 "Statement on Longer-Run Goals and Monetary Policy Strategy," often referred to as the "Consensus Statement."[90]

Considering current developments and to culminate its policy review, the FOMC published a revised Consensus Statement on August 27, 2020.[91] On its website, the Fed compared the current statement to the previous one. The big-deal change in the amended statement was that the FOMC now "judges that, following periods when inflation has been running persistently below 2 percent, appropriate monetary policy will likely aim to achieve inflation moderately above 2 percent for some time."[92]

In a speech on September 1, 2020, Fed Governor Lael Brainard, who was nominated and confirmed during the Obama administration, added an "F" to the beginning of the "AIT" acronym to reflect the "flexible" nature of the new approach:

> Flexible average inflation targeting (FAIT) is a consequential change in strategy. By committing to seek inflation that averages 2 percent over time, FAIT means that appropriate monetary policy would likely aim to achieve inflation moderately above 2 percent for a time to compensate for a period, such as the present, when it has been persistently below 2 percent. Consistent with this, I would expect the Committee to accommodate rather than offset inflationary pressures moderately above 2 percent, in a process of opportunistic reflation.[93]

Here's the rub: Given that the FOMC hadn't been able to get inflation up to 2.0% since January 2012, how could it realistically expect to overshoot that mark long enough for inflation to average 2.0%? The wishful thinking that underpins the FAIT concept is why we call the new approach "FAITH," or "flexible average inflation targeting hope"! FAITH may sound like a novel policy concept, but it's not. Former Fed Chair Ben Bernanke tossed around the idea of a similar shift in policy back in a 2017 Brookings blog post. And former Fed Chair Janet Yellen regularly commented that overshoots to inflation likely would be tolerated under her leadership.

In any event, what the policy change means in practical terms is greater likelihood that the Fed will keep interest rates close to zero for much longer than otherwise—even if employment conditions improve significantly and even if inflation rises to 2.0% or overshoots it for a while.

The Consensus Statement was previously revised by the FOMC on January 27, 2016 by referring to its inflation objective as a "symmetric inflation goal" rather than just an "inflation goal." The Statement added that the Committee "would be concerned if inflation were running persistently above or below this objective."[94] The phrase "symmetric inflation goal" was removed from the 2020 Statement.

The 2020 Statement reiterated the FOMC's commitment to the dual mandate. But the FOMC literally placed a heightened focus on achieving the employment goal by moving the discussion of employment ahead of inflation, i.e., higher up in the statement. The statement previously noted that maximum employment "may" be changeable and immeasurable, but "may" was removed in the 2020 statement. In other words, the FOMC now deemed maximum employment to be a subjective matter that can't be defined by a single variable such as the unemployment rate. Former Fed Chair Janet Yellen tracked a labor market dashboard with nine indicators of employment. Even though the unemployment situation seemed to be improving under her watch, she was troubled by relatively low labor force participation rates.

Importantly, "broad based" and "inclusive" were added as qualifiers to the maximum employment goal. Powell said that the revised statement "reflects our appreciation for the benefits of a strong labor market, particularly for many in low- and moderate-income communities." Powell often observed that the pandemic had complicated the employment situation considerably, making it much more challenging for workers who had lost their jobs to get them back.

Unpredictable Velocity

Monetarists—such as Milton Friedman, who were especially influential during the 1970s and 1980s—never doubted that inflation is always and everywhere a monetary phenomenon. Their certitude derived from their belief that inflation can be understood only in the context of the quantity theory of money, which is based on a deceptively simple equation: MV = PY.

This model assumes that the monetary authorities can determine the money supply (M) and that the velocity of money (V) is constant or at least predictable. If so, then they can drive nominal GDP (PY) and raise the price level (P) once real GDP (Y) is equal to or exceeds its noninflationary potential. By the way, they also need to have a constant or predictable money multiplier (m), i.e., the ratio of the broad money supply (M2) to the monetary base, which is currency plus bank reserves under the central bank's control.

Neither velocity nor the money multiplier have been constant, or even predictable, for a very long time, and even less so since the financial crisis of 2008. Velocity, defined as the ratio of nominal GDP to M2, has been on a downward trend since the late 1990s (*Fig. 39*). The money multiplier has also been unpredictable (*Fig. 40*). Since late 2008, the monetary base has soared thanks to the central banks' various QE programs, yet the growth rates in broad measures of the money supply have remained subdued as the money multiplier has plunged.

Nevertheless, the Fed's 2%-targeting approach, first announced at the end of January 2012, and later its FAITH-based version, which aims to overshoot the 2.0% target for periods of time, are predicated on the same flawed monetarist concept. Both the 2012 and 2020 versions of the Fed's Consensus Statements declare:

> The inflation rate over the longer run is primarily determined by monetary policy, and hence the Committee has the ability to specify a longer-run goal for inflation. The Committee reaffirms its judgment that inflation at the rate of 2 percent, as measured by the annual change in the price index for personal consumption expenditures, is most consistent over the longer run with the Federal Reserve's statutory mandate.

The 2020 version of this statement adds the following language:

> In order to anchor longer-term inflation expectations at this level, the Committee seeks to achieve inflation that averages 2 percent over time, and therefore judges that, following periods when inflation has been running persistently below 2 percent, appropriate monetary policy will likely aim to achieve inflation moderately above 2 percent for some time.

In my book *Fed Watching*, I predicted that FAITH might be the main result of the Fed's review of monetary policy. I wrote: "With all due respect, that's hilarious! Why do Fed officials want to embarrass themselves by targeting inflation over 2.0% when they haven't been able to move it up to 2.0% since officially targeting that level in January 2012?" Since then through late 2020, the headline inflation rate using the personal consumption expenditures deflator (PCED) has been tracking an annual trendline with a constant 1.3% growth rate. As a result, during November 2020, the PCED was 5.4% below where it would have been if it had been tracking 2.0% (*Fig. 41*).

To get back to the steeper trendline by the end of 2023, the PCED would have to increase by about 12%, or 4% per year! A longer catch-up period would moderate the needed inflation makeup. However, the open question remains: How will Fed officials boost inflation above 2.0% at all given that they haven't been able to get it even that high since 2012?

They must have FAITH that QE4ever and MMT will do what they were unable to achieve with QE1, QE2, and QE3. The latest round of QE certainly has boosted the growth rates of the major monetary aggregates. Through the end of December 2020, M2 rose 24.4% on a year-over-year basis, just below the mid-December record 26.0% pace (*Fig. 42*). If there is any pulse left in monetarism, surely this rapid pace of monetary growth should revive inflation. That could happen if both velocity and real GDP trace out V-shaped recoveries in 2021.

If inflation doesn't make a comeback, Fed officials may have to finally concede that inflation isn't solely a monetary phenomenon. The same can be said of the central bankers at the ECB and BOJ. During December, the headline and core CPI inflation rates, on a year-over-year basis, were -0.3% and 0.2% in the Eurozone and -1.2% and -1.0% in Japan (*Fig. 43* and *Fig. 44*).

Our money is still on the "4Ds," i.e., the four major deflationary forces. They should continue to keep a lid on inflation. Here are our current bottom lines on each of the 4Ds:

(1) *Détente.* In the grand sweep of economic history, inflation tends to occur during relatively short and infrequent episodes, i.e., during war times. The more common experience has been either very low inflation or outright deflation during peacetimes.

Periods of globalization follow wartimes. During peacetimes, national markets become increasingly integrated through trade and capital flows. The result is more global competition, which is inherently deflationary. The worsening Cold War between the US and China is a threat to globalization, but probably won't heat up to the point of causing inflation after the regime change that occurred in Washington, DC on January 20, 2021. In any event, China's exports during November edged back up to the record high, which was hit during July notwithstanding Trump's trade war with that country.

(2) *Technological Disruption.* Nevertheless, recent global trade tensions and the pandemic are likely to cause businesses to diversify their offshore supply chains away from China and to onshore more of them. That could be costly and inflationary. Alternatively, it could be cost effective now that labor shortages attributable to global demographic trends are stimulating technological innovations in automation, robotics, artificial intelligence,

3D manufacturing, and 5G telecommunications. These all enable onshoring and boost productivity to boot.

Nonfarm productivity jumped 4.0% year over year during the third quarter of 2020, the fastest pace since the first quarter of 2010. We are expecting a secular rebound in productivity growth during the Roaring 2020s. So far, so good: The 20-quarter growth rate of productivity (at an annual rate) rose from a recent low of 0.6% during the fourth quarter of 2015 to 1.7% during the third quarter of 2020. We believe that the pandemic accelerated the pace of applying new technologies to boost efficiency and profit margins.

(3) *Demographics.* Fertility rates have plunged below population replacement in recent decades around the world as urbanization has changed the economics of having children. Instead of being an important source of labor and elder care, as they are in agrarian communities, children are all cost in urban settings. Nursing homes have few vacancies, while maternity wards have plenty. Increasingly geriatric demographic profiles are inherently deflationary, in our opinion.

(4) *Debt.* During the 1960s through the 1980s, debt was stimulative; more of it stimulated more demand and added to inflationary pressures. Now, easy credit conditions aren't as stimulative to demand as in the past because so many consumers have so much debt already. However, easy monetary conditions are a lifeline to zombie companies, enabling them to raise funds to stay in business, adding to global supplies of goods and services, which is deflationary. (For a summary, see the excerpt from my 2020 book titled *Four Deflationary Forces Keeping a Lid on Inflation.*[95])

Some Like It Hot

On October 14, 2016, then-Fed Chair Janet Yellen gave a speech at a conference sponsored by the Boston Fed and attended by Fed and academic economists. The topic of discussion: "The Elusive 'Great' Recovery: Causes and Implications for Future Business Cycle Dynamics." Her talk was titled "Macroeconomic Research After the Crisis."[96] It was a remarkable speech that should have been titled "Macroeconomic Research in Crisis." The unemployment rate had dropped from a peak of 10.0% during October 2009 to 4.9% in August 2016. The Fed had hiked interest rates once at the end of 2015 and was going to do so again at the end of 2016. Yellen explained why such gradual normalization of monetary policy made sense.

She talked about "hysteresis," the idea that persistent shortfalls in aggregate demand could adversely affect the supply side of the economy. Then she rhetorically asked: "If we assume that hysteresis is in fact present to some degree after deep recessions, the natural next question is to ask whether it might be possible to reverse these adverse supply-side effects by temporarily running a 'high-pressure economy,' with robust aggregate demand and a tight labor market." My commentary on her speech was titled "Some Like It Hot." I concluded that Yellen was in no hurry to rush the pace of rate hikes.

The 2020 FAITH statement clearly gives more weight to maximizing employment than to keeping a 2.0% lid on inflation. Under Fed Chair Powell, the Fed is likely to try to heat up the economy to overcome the GVC-induced hysteresis.

Chapter 6
Financial Stability

The Third Mandate

The Fed's August 27, 2020 FAITH statement included a couple of new sentences about maintaining financial stability. This topic was never mentioned before in the annual statement on inflation targeting that was first released at the beginning of 2012. Here is the specific addition:

> Moreover, sustainably achieving maximum employment and price stability depends on a stable financial system. Therefore, the Committee's policy decisions reflect its longer-run goals, its medium-term outlook, and its assessments of the balance of risks, including risks to the financial system that could impede the attainment of the Committee's goals.

In my book *Fed Watching*, I described financial stability as the Fed's third mandate. However, unlike the dual mandate, it isn't required by a congressional act. Nevertheless, it is the Fed's very reason for existing. The Federal Reserve System was created by the 1913 Federal Reserve Act, enacted largely in response to the Panic of 1907. The hope was that the Fed could provide financial stability and prevent future financial crises from harming the economy via an "elastic currency." The Fed's original mandate, therefore, wasn't to moderate the business cycle but rather to stabilize the financial system.

William McChesney Martin was Fed chair from April 2, 1951 until January 31, 1970, serving under five Presidents. He famously said that the Fed "is in the position of the chaperone who has ordered the punch bowl removed just when the party was really warming up." Here is the full quote from his October 19, 1955 speech:

> In the field of monetary and credit policy, precautionary action to prevent inflationary excesses is bound to have some onerous effects—if it did not it would be ineffective and futile. Those who have the task of making such policy don't expect you to applaud. The Federal Reserve, as one writer put it, after the recent increase in the discount rate, is in the position of the chaperone who has ordered the punch bowl removed just when the party was really warming up.

He wisely added:

> But a note should be made here that, while money policy can do a great deal, it is by no means all powerful. In other words, we should not place too heavy a burden on monetary policy. It must be accompanied by appropriate fiscal and budgetary measures if we are to achieve our aim of stable progress. If we ask too much of monetary policy, we will not only fail but we will also discredit this useful, and indeed indispensable, tool for shaping our economic development. [97]

Following World War II, it was widely feared that the US economy could fall into another depression. Congress passed the Employment Act of 1946, directing the federal government to promote maximum employment, production, and purchasing power. Back then, liberals wanted to call it "The Full Employment Act," but conservatives resisted. In early 1975, Congress adopted Resolution 133, instructing the Federal Reserve to, among other things: "maintain long run growth of the monetary and credit aggregates commensurate with economy's long run potential to increase production, so as to promote effectively the goals of maximum employment, stable prices, and moderate long-term interest rates."[98]

In 1977, Congress amended the Federal Reserve Act to incorporate the provisions of Resolution 133 in the Full Employment and Balanced Growth Act, known informally as the "Humphrey–Hawkins Full Employment Act." It was signed into law by President Jimmy Carter on October 27, 1978. This act calls on the federal government to strive for full employment, production growth, price stability, and balanced trade and budget accounts. The Fed is specifically mandated to maintain long-run economic growth and minimize inflation. Fed officials believe that this legislation imposes a dual mandate on the Fed to keep the unemployment rate low and consistent with full employment, while achieving inflation so low that it amounts to price stability. The law requires the semiannual congressional testimony and monetary policy report by the chair.

In response to the GFC and the Great Recession, Fed Chair Ben Bernanke (from 2006 through early 2014) believed that the dual mandate unambiguously required ultra-easy monetary policy, with the federal funds rate pegged near zero and lots of QE. Bernanke wanted to do everything in the Fed's power to keep the punch bowl full for as long as it took to get the party going again. All that liquidity did get the party going again in asset markets, as the prices of stocks, bonds, and real estate rebounded sharply during the 2010s.

However, the economic expansion remained lackluster, as did the recovery in the labor market. So Fed Chair Janet Yellen (from 2014 to early 2018) also continued to provide plenty of punch, though she cut back on the rum a bit, as the labor market improved during her term as Fed chair. In her opinion, the dual mandate required a gradual normalization of monetary policy.

Powell stayed on the course charted by Yellen during 2018 and 2019, adding more rum to the punch bowl when deemed appropriate—though it seemed to be provided mostly to keep the party in the stock market from fizzling out.

The dual mandate has led to significant financial instability. Fed officials should reassess their assumption that moderating the business cycle should be their main job. Working under that assumption, they tend inadvertently to cause financial instability. That's because lenders and borrowers take on too much risk when they feel assured by the Fed's actions that recessions are unlikely to happen and that any that do occur will be short and shallow. A good rum punch can easily promote that delusory assurance.

It was good to see that the Fed started to monitor financial stability more formally in late 2018, with regular reports on it. However, the dual mandate is required by law—financial stability isn't. That doesn't mean that Fed officials can't work around that by arguing that achieving the dual mandate requires financial stability, as they did in the 2020 FAITH statement.

Postponing the Zombie Apocalypse

The Fed issued its first-ever *Financial Stability Report* (*FSR*) on November 28, 2018.[99] The stated purpose of this semi-annual report is "to promote public understanding and increase transparency and accountability for the Federal Reserve's views on this topic." The report explained that the adverse events that occurred during the GFC were dramatically worsened by an unstable financial system.

The first report was balanced, with some vulnerabilities flagged as potentially troublesome and others as less concerning. No clear and present dangers were identified. The report suggested that the Fed was somewhat worried about elevated asset valuations and levels of corporate borrowing but unconcerned about household borrowing, financial sector leverage, and funding risks.

There were two more reports during 2019 before the pandemic. The May report had the same don't-worry-we-are-on-it tone as the first report. However, credit quality had clearly deteriorated in the corporate bond market. The Fed observed that during the first quarter of 2019, the share of nonfinancial, investment-grade bonds rated at the lowest investment-grade level (for example, an S&P rating of triple-B) reached near-record levels. A little more than 50% of investment-grade bonds outstanding were rated triple-B, amounting to about $1.9 trillion.[100]

The Fed's third *Financial Stability Report* was dated November 2019. Like the previous two, it was relatively sanguine, but did warn about the mounting debts of nonfinancial corporations and their potential to destabilize the financial system. The report also acknowledged that historically low interest rates could undermine the stability of the financial sector: "If interest rates were to remain low for a prolonged period, the profitability of banks, insurers, and other financial intermediaries could come under stress and spur reach-for-yield behavior, thereby increasing the vulnerability of the financial sector to subsequent shocks."[101]

Also, just before the pandemic, the International Monetary Fund (IMF) published its October 2019 *Global Financial Stability Report (GFSR)* titled "Lower for Longer." At the time, we observed that it should have been titled "Is a Zombie Apocalypse Coming?" given the report's disturbing conclusion: "In a material economic slowdown scenario, half as severe as the global financial crisis, corporate debt-at-risk (debt owed by firms that cannot cover their interest expenses with their earnings) could rise to $19 trillion—or nearly 40 percent of total corporate debt in major economies, and above post-crisis levels."[102]

Just before Halloween 2019 and before the GVC 2020, Powell was asked at his October 30, 2019 press conference about the IMF's latest *GFSR*. After implying that everything is mostly hunky-dory, Powell said: "That leaves businesses, which is where the issue has been. Leverage among corporations and other forms of business, private businesses, is historically high. We've been monitoring it carefully and taking appropriate steps."[103]

That was Powell's "trick or trick." He didn't say what steps had been taken, unless he meant the three cuts in the federal funds rate during the second half of 2019, which had stoked a reach-for-yield frenzy by investors. That meant that zombie companies could continue to refinance and to raise funds in the bond market at attractive rates. So the Fed was extending their lives and increasing their numbers, postponing the zombie apocalypse rather than taking any steps to keep it from happening.

The Fed's next *FSR*, released in May 2020, warned that conditions in the corporate bond market, which had been worrisome in 2019, had gotten worse as a result of the pandemic in early 2020. It noted that almost $125 billion of nonfinancial investment-grade corporate debt had been downgraded to speculative grade since late February and "expected defaults may rise if the economic outlook and corporate earnings are revised downward."

That could worsen the credit crunch if institutional investors with minimum credit ratings mandates were forced to sell downgraded bonds. The *FSR* noted:

> Against this backdrop, approximately $170 billion of investment-grade corporate bonds and $29 billion of speculative-grade corporate bonds issued by nonfinancial corporations are set to mature before the end of 2020, representing 25 percent and 11 percent, respectively, of the average annual nonfinancial corporate issuance of each grade over the past five years.[104]

The preliminary damage assessment offered by the Fed's May 2020 *Financial Stability Report* concluded:

> While the financial regulatory reforms adopted since 2008 have substantially increased the resilience of the financial sector, the financial system nonetheless amplified the shock, and financial sector vulnerabilities are likely to be significant in the near term. The strains on household and business balance sheets from the economic and financial shocks since March will likely create fragilities that last for some time. Financial institutions—including the banking sector, which had large capital and liquidity buffers before the shock—may experience strains as a result.

As we discussed in Chapter 4, during February and March of 2020 the pandemic unleashed a mad dash for cash and a severe, but short, credit crunch. It was short because of the Fed's March 23 response to the crisis. That response involved purchasing $2.4 trillion in US Treasuries and MBSs since then through the end of 2020. The Fed also provided loans via several liquidity facilities. This lending jumped from $383 billion during the March 11 week to a high of $1.22 trillion during the week of May 13, 2020. As the financial panic abated, the liquidity facilities' loans fell to $566 billion during the December 30 week. But some of the Fed's lending facilities authorized by the CARES Act were barely used, mostly because QE4ever calmed the financial markets quickly and dramatically.

Lo and behold: The Fed's fourth *Financial Stability Report*, dated November 2020, reported that the Fed's rapid response to the pandemic had worked to stop the credit crunch, especially in the bond market:

> The announcements of the PMCCF, SMCCF, and MLF [Municipal Liquidity Facility] in late March and early April led to rapid improvements in corporate and municipal bond

markets well ahead of the facilities' actual opening. Spreads across a variety of debt markets quickly narrowed, permitting businesses and municipalities to borrow at sharply lower costs . . . . SMCCF purchases to date amount to about $13 billion—just more than 0.2 percent of the $5.5 trillion of outstanding nonfinancial corporate bonds. The MLF has, to date, purchased two issues totaling just more than $1.6 billion. However, since the announcement of the backstop facilities and funding market stabilization measures, more than $1 trillion in new nonfinancial corporate bonds and more than $250 billion in municipal debt have been issued, purchased almost entirely by the private sector . . . .

Credit quality, which had deteriorated significantly along with revenues and earnings during the spring of 2020, stabilized during the summer, the November 2020 *FSR* observed. Nevertheless, at the end of the third quarter, about half of nonfinancial investment-grade debt outstanding was rated in the lowest category of the investment-grade range (triple-B)—near an all-time high.

Commercial banks also experienced a deterioration in the quality of their loans but were projected to remain well capitalized. The November 2020 *FSR* reported: "Allowances for loan losses surged in the first half of 2020 as large banks implemented the current expected credit losses (CECL) accounting standard and reassessed their losses (especially in credit card loans and corporate lending) in light of the COVID-19 shock." Under CECL accounting standards, banks are required to set aside provisions for the expected losses over the life of a loan.[105] The Fed's weekly commercial bank report showed that allowances for loan and lease losses at all commercial banks jumped by $106 billion from the last week in February through the end of 2020 (*Fig. 45*).

On June 25, after releasing the results of its bank stress tests for 2020, the Fed placed prohibitions on share buybacks and a cap on dividend payments by 34 banks with more than $100 billion in assets.[106] Fed Governor Lael Brainard objected to the fact that banks were still allowed to pay out dividends in any fashion. "The payouts will amount to a depletion of loss-absorbing capital," she wrote in a statement. "This is inconsistent with the purpose of the stress tests, which is to be forward-looking by preserving resilience, not backward-looking by authorizing payouts based on net income from past quarters that had already been paid out."[107]

The restrictions, imposed for the third quarter, were due to expire September 30 but were extended through the end of the year.[108] On Friday, December 18, the Fed released the results of another stress test on the banks.[109] The press release announced that the Fed would allow the nation's biggest banks to resume share buybacks in the first quarter of 2021. Dividends would continue to be capped, with the total of a bank's dividends and repurchases in the first quarter not to exceed the average quarterly profit from the four most recent quarters.[110]

The central message from the Fed's November 2020 *FSR* was that the pandemic could have triggered a financial meltdown and a depression, but, thankfully, monetary policy averted these calamities.

Plunge Protection Team

On March 18, 1988, in the wake of the stock market crash of 1987, then-President Ronald Reagan created the Working Group on Financial Markets by executive order.[111] Its original purpose was to report specifically on the Black Monday events of October 19, 1987, when the S&P 500 plunged 20.5% in just one day, and to recommend measures to avoid a similar plunge in the future. The group is headed by the secretary of the Treasury; other members include the chair of the Board of Governors of the Federal

Reserve, the chair of the Securities and Exchange Commission, and the chair of the Commodity Futures Trading Commission (or the aides or officials they designate to represent them). It came to be called the "Plunge Protection Team" (PPT), a phrase coined by *The Washington Post* in 1997.[112]

The February 15, 1999 issue of *Time* featured a story titled "The Committee to Save the World: The inside story of how the Three Marketeers have prevented a global economic meltdown— so far." Pictured on the front cover were two PPT members, Fed Chair Alan Greenspan and Treasury Secretary Robert Rubin, along with Deputy Secretary of the Treasury Larry Summers. That same year, all three had supported legislation to deregulate the credit derivatives market, which arguably set the stage for the GFC and Great Recession of 2008![113]

Following the onset of the pandemic, global central bankers and fiscal authorities took unprecedented monetary and fiscal policy actions to serve as a "Bridge to Recovery." That is the title of Chapter 1 of the IMF's October 2020 *GFSR*. Our short interpretation of the chapter's main point is that policy actions have saved financial markets but have disconnected markets from underlying economic fundamentals, and that has elevated global financial risk.

The report states that the pandemic response measures implemented by the central banks worked to calm global stock markets despite the ongoing uncertainty of the pandemic. Indeed, market performance would likely have been much weaker without their unprecedented level of policy support. Major factors that could cause renewed problems for the financial markets were the anticipation of decreased policy support and a delayed recovery, according to the IMF. Nevertheless, the report attributed the containment of near-term global financial risks "for now" to the unprecedented global policy response. But the report also warned that the policies that had saved the world might lead to excessive risk-taking.[114]

Recalling *Time*'s February 15, 1999 cover, we thought a more apropos title for the IMF report would have been "The Central Bankers Who Saved the World." It could have featured photos of the world's major central bank heads. Along the same lines, we think the Fed's November 2020 *FSR* could have been titled "Mission Nearly Accomplished" and featured the famous photo of Fed Chair Jerome Powell and Treasury Secretary Steven Mnuchin wearing face masks and elbow bumping after a hearing of the House of Representatives Financial Services Committee on Tuesday, June 30, 2020.[115] Indeed, the *FSR*'s central message was that calamitous pandemic repercussions had been prevented by monetary policy, and fiscal policy—represented by Treasury Secretary Mnuchin—clearly helped too. Powell and Mnuchin indeed were a two-man PPT. Together, they succeeded in ending the 33.9% plunge in the S&P 500 over the 33 days from February 19 through March 23. They stopped the credit crunch that occurred over roughly the same period. Their joint policies contributed to the V-shaped rebound in the economy during 2020.

Proof of their accomplishment was in the Fed's lending activities. These were almost nonexistent. The lender of last resort wasn't doing the volume of lending during the pandemic that it had promised. Compared to the potential size of purchases, the transactions were minimal.

As of November 30, the PMCCF was operational but had not yet closed any transactions, according to the Fed's credit facilities update on December 10, 2020. The Fed did start purchasing corporate-bond ETFs through the SMCCF. As of November 30, the total outstanding amount of the Fed's loans under the SMCCF was only $13.7 billion.[116]

The total outstanding loans under the Fed's other facilities reached their highest level of just $97.7 billion as of June 30. On November 30, 2020, the latest update as of this writing, actual loans totaled about $72.0 billion out of the $1.55 trillion in lending capacity. On October 30, 2020, the Fed adjusted the terms of the MSLP to better target support to smaller businesses and nonprofit organizations, including to lower the minimum loan size and to update the transaction, loan origination, and loan-servicing fee terms for smaller loans. While the scale of MSLP lending increased to $6.0 billion by November 30, up from $4.0 billion as of October 31, the utilization remained nowhere near capacity. On December 29, the Fed extended the termination date of the MSLP to January 8, 2021 with approval from the Secretary of the Treasury to allow more time to process and fund loans that were submitted on or before December 14.

Of note, according to the related transaction spreadsheet, the MLF included loans to just two entities: The State of Illinois and the New York Metropolitan Transportation Authority.

In a November 19 letter, Treasury Secretary Mnuchin made headlines by asking Fed Chair Powell for his money back.[117] Mnuchin essentially argued that markets had responded so well to the commitment of T-Fed to provide financial support that much of it was no longer necessary.

When the Fed made emergency loans to nonbank financial institutions in 2008 to stem the financial crisis, it did so under the auspices of Section 13(3) of the Federal Reserve Act, which was added at the height of the Great Depression in 1932. It expanded the Fed's emergency-lending authority beyond the financial sector to include a broader set of institutions.[118] The new section allowed the Fed to act as a lender of last resort during "unusual and exigent" circumstances, i.e., when credit markets experienced a meltdown during a financial crisis.[119]

The Fed's emergency powers had been curtailed after the Fed rescued AIG during the 2008 GFC. Congress passed legislation mandating that any Fed rescue package had to be broad-based and not aimed at one company, and also had to be approved beforehand by the Treasury secretary.

During December 2020, Senator Pat Toomey (R–PA) added language to another pandemic relief bill. This bill related to Fed lending programs set up earlier that year, especially to state and local governments, and the new language added the requirement of congressional approval. The compromise bill that was enacted required the Fed to get approval from Congress to expand its purchases of municipal securities, but did not cut off its power to help states and companies in the future. It did, however, bar the Fed from reviving the same facilities used in 2020.

In his letter, Mnuchin wrote Powell: "I would like to personally thank you and the entire team at the Federal Reserve for the great work in establishing 13 separate credit facilities pursuant to section 13(3) of the Federal reserve Act and the Board's Regulation A." He noted that on March 17, he approved the establishment of the CPFF (with $10 billion from the ESF) and the PDCF (without ESF funds). On March 18, he approved the establishment of the MMLF (with $10 billion from the ESF). Under the March 27 CARES Act, Congress allocated $454 billion to the Treasury to contribute to Fed liquidity facilities. Mnuchin approved $195 billion of these funds for the PMCCF, SMCCF, MLF, MSLP, and TALF. Mnuchin observed:

> Across these facilities, the Treasury commitment combined with Federal Reserve funding would have allowed approximately $2 trillion of lending capacity. Currently $25 billion of loans and other assets have been funded, which is substantially below Treasury's capital commitment. Fortunately, with the announcement of significant financial support, markets

responded positively, spreads tightened, and banks continued lending. The Federal Reserve facilities supported by the Treasury's contribution of CARES Act funds have clearly achieved their objective.

Mnuchin reviewed all the progress that had been made in the financial markets. He observed that the liquidity facilities were due to expire at the end of 2020. He asked for the Fed to extend CPFF, MMLF, PDCF, and PPPLF for another 90 days.[120] However, he asked the Fed to return $455 billion that had mostly been appropriated under the CARES Act to backstop five of the facilities. Powell agreed to do so in a November 20 letter to Mnuchin.[121]

Did Mnuchin's move suggest that T-Fed had a very short life from only March 23 through November 19? Not really. As Powell himself acknowledged, the Fed had crossed lots of red lines. Everyone in Washington knew that. The Fed had been politicized more than ever. From the vantage point of early 2021, it appeared that the Treasury and the Fed were set to work more closely than ever now with Janet Yellen as Treasury secretary in the new Biden administration. When Yellen was the Fed chair, Powell was the vice-chair; they had a history of working well together. Like all those corporate zombies, T-Fed will live to die another day.

In any event, a new PPT of sorts once again in 2020 protected us from a credit crunch and a recession, just as the original PPT policymakers had done. They did so by pushing interest rates down to record lows, flooding the financial markets with liquidity through QE4ever, boosting government social benefits dramatically, and promising to catch the fallen angels and feed the zombies if necessary. However, have all these interventions set the stage for the next stock market meltup, followed by the next stock market meltdown?

Mother of All Meltups?

Interestingly, the ECB warned in a May 26, 2020 press release that according to its latest *Financial Stability Report*, the pandemic increased the risks to financial stability. These included "richly valued asset prices, fragile investment funds, the sustainability of sovereign and corporate debt, and weak bank profitability." The report reassuringly concluded that the ECB's policies had helped to stabilize market conditions. The report added that the Eurozone's various fiscal stimulus packages were expected to support the region's economy by helping corporations to sustain cash flow.[122]

By comparison, the Fed's November 2020 *FSR* seemed downright relaxed about financial instability. The report acknowledged that asset prices in various markets were at "elevated levels." However, that "likely reflected the low level of Treasury yields." In any event, very low Treasury yields explained why corporate bond yields were down to historically low levels. Yield spreads between corporate bonds and comparable-maturity Treasury bonds narrowed considerably to their historical averages. Home prices continued rising to record highs, but the Fed's report observed: "Nationwide, prices appear to be a little above their long-run average relationship with property rents."[123] Nothing to worry about. After all, asset prices should be supported by "a stronger-than-expected economic recovery" thanks to "prompt and forceful policy responses—including fiscal stimulus, lower interest rates, and various asset purchase and emergency lending programs," the report added. Our reaction when we read this was: "Go, T-Fed! You rock!"

In his last press conference of 2020, Powell was asked by CNBC's Jeff Cox whether he was "concerned about asset valuations in light of the highly accommodative Fed policies?" Powell acknowledged that P/Es are "historically high." He added that may not be relevant "in a world where we think the 10-year Treasury [yield] is going to be lower than it has been historically . . ." So stocks are "not overpriced." In addition, Powell observed that, as a result of low interest rates, "companies have been able to handle their debt loads even in a weak period." He noted that debt defaults and downgrades have declined since early 2020. He concluded that he doesn't see "a lot of red flags."[124]

So Powell's answer to the important question posed by Cox was that asset valuations are fine since interest rates are so low. The question that he dodged was whether asset valuations were getting too frothy *because* the Fed was promising to keep interest rates too low for too long, as Powell's answer implied was the Fed's intention.

Powell's answer indicated that the Fed's solution to the zombie problem was no solution at all. The Fed exacerbated the problem of zombie companies by allowing corporations to borrow at record-low interest rates as investors continued to reach for yield. As investors purchased the bonds of these dodgy companies that would have been buried but for the Fed's remarkably easy credit conditions, the can was simply kicked down the road!

The result, as we noted in Chapter 2, was the record issuance of corporate bonds during 2020. Bond yields should have been rising during the second half of 2020 according to the ratio of the price of copper to the price of gold and according to the manufacturing PMI. Both variables had been highly correlated with the bond yield in the past and suggested that it should have been closer to 2.00% than to 1.00% by the end of 2020. The Fed was clearly keeping a lid on the yield, as evidenced by the fact that the Fed was purchasing Treasury notes and bonds almost as fast as the Treasury was issuing them from March 23 through the end of 2020.

So, stocks weren't irrationally exuberant; rather, they were rationally discounting the fact that the Fed would keep the bond yield low for a very long time, as Powell continued to promise! In our opinion, he was inadvertently setting the stage for another meltup, just as Fed Chair Alan Greenspan had done in the second half of the 1990s.

Recall that in his December 5, 1996 speech, Greenspan famously asked, "But how do we know when irrational exuberance has unduly escalated asset values, which then become subject to unexpected and prolonged contractions . . . ?" Initially, at the time, the widespread interpretation was that the Fed chair thought that valuations were too high. But it soon became obvious that he was simply asking the question and that he wasn't convinced that stocks were too expensive. Even in his speech, he supported the bullish case by observing, "Clearly, sustained low inflation implies less uncertainty about the future, and lower risk premiums imply higher prices of stocks and other earning assets."[125] Now, Powell was saying that record-low interest rates implied lower risk premiums and higher prices of stocks and other earnings assets.

Inflation stayed low during the late 1990s and stock prices soared along with valuation multiples. Following the selloff triggered by the Russian default crisis and the collapse of Long-Term Capital Management, the S&P 500 and Nasdaq soared 59.6% and 255.8% from their 1998 lows through their tops in March 2000 (*Fig. 46*). This time, since March 23, they were up 67.9% and 87.9% through the end of 2020, respectively.

Powell's comments during his December 16 press conference were an invitation to party like it's 1999 because he would keep the punch bowl full and spiked! He'd do so until the pandemic was over—which could take a while. As he observed in his prepared remarks, "Recent news on vaccines has been very positive. However, significant challenges and uncertainties remain with regard to the timing, production, and distribution of vaccines, as well as their efficacy across different groups." He warned, "It remains difficult to assess the timing and scope of the economic implications of these developments. The ongoing surge in new Covid-19 cases, both here in the United States and abroad, is particularly concerning, and the next few months are likely to be very challenging." But, don't worry, the Fed will keep interest rates near zero.

During 2020, the forward P/E of the S&P 500 fell from 19.0 on February 19 to 12.9 on March 23. By the end of the year, it was up to 22.5. It was highly correlated with the size of the Fed's balance sheet (*Fig. 47*) The weekly Buffett Ratio of the S&P 500 stock price index to the index's forward revenues closed the year at 2.59, the highest since the start of the data during January 2004 (*Fig. 48*).[126]

There were lots of other signs of irrational exuberance in the stock market at the end of 2020. The market for initial public offerings was red hot. Emerging market stock prices were on fire, which happens when the Fed is expected to keep monetary conditions easy. Stock and bond prices had melted up since the Fed started pouring liquidity into the financial markets. Stock prices seemed poised for a continuation of the meltup as we went to press at the end of 2020, thanks to Powell's assurances. The "Mother of All Meltups" seemed to be underway.

The Governor's 2013 Speech

Before we move on, let's look back at Powell's June 27, 2013 speech titled "Thoughts on Unconventional Monetary Policy."[127] At the time, he was a Fed governor. He said that he supported QE1, the first round of Fed purchases of securities starting during November 2008. QE1 had "contributed significantly to ending the financial crisis and preventing a much more severe economic contraction." He also endorsed QE2, the second round of purchases that began in November 2010. It "also appears to have been successful in countering disinflationary pressures."

He was much less enthusiastic about QE3, which started during September 2012. He acknowledged the benefits of continuing the purchases. However, he also warned about the potential costs. First and foremost, Powell was worried about the risks of causing financial instability. He said:

> One concern is that our policies might drive excessive risk-taking or create bubbles in financial assets or housing. A related worry is that the eventual process of reducing purchases and normalizing the balance sheet may itself be destabilizing or disruptive to the economy. Indeed, recent volatility in markets is in part related to concerns about the possibility of a reduction in asset purchases.

Just as Greenspan had done in his December 5, 1996 speech, Powell wondered whether the Fed's policies during 2013 "could be encouraging irrational expectations of high returns." Then, he asked, "Is there any sign of that now?" He didn't see any in the equity market, but "there have been signs of a 'reach for yield' in the fixed-income markets for some time."

Yet at the end of 2020, Powell's spin was that equity valuations weren't stretched given that interest rates were so low. There were certainly lots more signs of irrational exuberance in the equity market and of reaching for yield in the bond market late in 2020 than there were back in 2013.

We should add that in his 2013 speech, Powell also warned "that the process of normalizing monetary policy and the balance sheet could itself be destabilizing or disruptive to the economy." During the three previous QE programs, Fed officials often discussed how they would normalize monetary policy once the economy required less support from monetary policy. This time, neither Powell nor any of his colleagues were discussing the Fed's exit strategy at the end of 2020.

Chapter 7

Free Money Theory

The Wizard of Oz

We live in surreal times. In Chapter 1, we compared them to the TV series *The Twilight Zone*. However, a more apt comparison would be with the land that Dorothy and her dog Toto visited in the movie *The Wizard of Oz*. When a tornado ripped her house from its foundation, causing it to crash-land in Oz, she emerged safe and sound, looked around in wonder and famously marveled, "Toto, I've a feeling we're not in Kansas anymore."

The analogy with Oz was recently provided by none other than the Wizard of MMT, Professor Stephanie Kelton. In her June 2020 book *The Deficit Myth: Modern Monetary Theory and the Birth of the People's Economy*, she wrote: "Like Dorothy and her companions in *The Wizard of Oz*, we need to see through the myths and remember once again that we've had the power all along."[128]

Kelton was referring to Dorothy's power to go back home to Kansas simply by clicking the heels of her ruby-red slippers three times. Similarly, Kelton believes that the US government has always had the power to run huge budget deficits and should be doing so now to cure all our ills. As a result of the GVC, her theory took on a life of its own. Governments around the world spent massively on stimulative deficit-financed fiscal policies to offset the recessionary forces unleashed by the GVC. Central bankers provided ultra-easy monetary policies to allow the resulting deficits to be financed at record low interest rates.

Until 2020, MMT was an offbeat school of thought. As we noted in the Introduction, it isn't modern, isn't monetary, and isn't a theory. We prefer to call it "Free Money Theory." Its advocates argue that when sovereign governments borrow in a national currency that they alone issue, that debt has no risk of default, as the governments can always print more money to make good on future promises. MMT suggests that governments can borrow without limits until inflation becomes a problem. Inflation becomes a problem only when resources become so constrained that prices rise.

As described in Chapter 2, on Friday, March 27, four days after the Fed's QE4ever announcement, Trump signed the CARES Act. It provided $2.2 trillion in rescue programs for the economy, including $454 billion for the US Treasury to provide as capital to the Fed to make $4 trillion in loans through various SPVs. In other words, the US federal government implemented an untested theory on a grand scale.

Kelton is one of the most vocal proponents of MMT today. She is a former chief economist on the US Senate Budget Committee and professor of economics and public policy at Stony Brook University. Her book reads like the MMT movement's manifesto.

Kelton argues that the federal government can and should run large budget deficits as long as inflation remains subdued. MMT opponents' main objection is that the theory provides a blank check for the government to get much bigger. It provides the government with too much power to allocate resources. Free-market capitalists believe that markets do a much better job of allocating resources than politicians and bureaucrats. Kelton clearly disagrees; but before we go there, let's dive into her theoretical description of MMT.

The central premise of MMT is that the US federal government, as the exclusive issuer of its sovereign currency (i.e., the US dollar), can "print" money without limit. It can do so as necessary to service or to pay down the public debt. It follows, therefore, that there is no well-defined limit on deficit-financed government spending unless and until inflation heats up.

Kelton notes: "Both the US Treasury and its fiscal agent, the Federal Reserve, have the authority to issue the US dollar. This might involve minting the coins in your pocket, printing up the bills in your wallet, or creating digital dollars known as reserves that exist only as electronic entries on bank balance sheets."[129]

The power of the monetary printing press is not limited to the US. Any country that issues and borrows in its own currency also has the power of MMT.

Kelton contends that government budget deficits only matter if they cause inflation. That happens when real resources in the economy are strained by "overspending," which causes inflation. The clear implication is that federal government deficits can balloon until they cause inflation to heat up. Kelton believes that the federal government budget deficit clearly is too small if there is any unemployment, a sign of underutilized resources.

MMT maintains that the federal government can achieve both full employment and stable inflation with an appropriate amount of deficit-financed spending. But what happens when the economy hits the wall of full utilization of resources, causing inflation to heat up? Any additional government spending beyond full resource utilization is inflationary. But never fear: MMT theorizes that inflation can easily be taxed away!

The old-school Keynesian concept of running budget deficits during recessions and surpluses during expansions is so yesterday. Even modern-school Keynesians have long abandoned any notion of fiscal discipline during good times. New school MMTers reject the Keynesian belief—held by central bankers around the world—that a certain amount of unemployment is necessary to keep inflation stable. That concept is often referred to as the "natural rate of unemployment" or "Non-Accelerating Inflation Rate of Unemployment" (NAIRU). MMT advocates dismiss NAIRU given their stance that it's possible to balance full employment (i.e., literally zero unemployment) with stable inflation. If done right, the theory goes, MMT can take the resources that are underutilized in the private sector and put them to work in the public sector.

From an MMT point of view, "we should rely on adjustments in taxes and spending (fiscal policy) rather than interest rates (monetary policy)" to balance our economy.[130] Kelton argues, as Keynesians do, that fiscal policy is better equipped for this task than monetary policy, mainly because the Federal Reserve cannot force borrowing to boost spending; it can only reduce the cost of borrowing. Fiscal spending directly targets areas of the private sector that need a boost.

MMT is based on an accounting identity, as every surplus (deficit) in one sector of the economy is offset by a deficit (surplus) in another sector of the economy. According to MMT, there are three main "buckets" in the economy: the public sector, the private sector, and the foreign sector. The financial balance for any of these sectors at a given time all must total to zero. As Kelton observes: "Fiscal surpluses suck money out of the [private] economy. Fiscal deficits do the opposite."[131]

Fiscal deficits also serve to keep the US private sector from falling into a deficit when the foreign sector runs at a surplus, Kelton maintains. More specifically, "the government must run budget deficits that exceed the US trade deficit."[132] The US consistently runs a trade deficit with the foreign sector as it imports more than it exports, bringing in goods and services and sending US dollars abroad.

For years, Congress has followed three main rules when it comes to the federal budget: PAYGO, the Byrd Rule, and the deficit ceiling. In 2018, Congress, led by Speaker Nancy Pelosi (D-CA), reinstituted PAYGO, or "Pay As You Go," to "demonstrate their commitment to good, old fashioned household budgeting."[133] With PAYGO, federal borrowing to finance new expenditures is not permitted. So lawmakers must cover any new spending pro-posals with revenue from new taxes. Under the Byrd rule, on the Senate side, deficits can increase, but not beyond a 10-year budget window. Finally, the debt ceiling puts a legal limit on the allowable federal government debt. Kelton points out that while these rules may be politically useful, they are completely artificial. She says: "Because all of these constraints were imposed by Congress, they can all be waived or suspended by Congress."[134]

Kelton promotes lots of controversial policy prescriptions based on MMT. "The question is," she writes, "How do we want the federal government to use its great power? . . . Can we trust Congress to make the right choices, at the right time, making pro-ductive choices when there is fiscal space and exercising the nec-essary restraint as resources become scarce?"[135]

Kelton's readers can easily detect her political leanings. Her agenda focuses on how the nation's real resources should be allo-cated by government programs rather than how extensive and big those programs should be or how they should be financed. Kelton contends that, rather than focusing on the fiscal deficit, politicians should focus on the real deficits in our economy. According to Kelton, these deficits can be addressed with fiscal policies (and spending) as follows: a good-jobs deficit (a minimum standard of living), a household-savings deficit (free higher education and affordable childcare), a healthcare deficit (insurance for all and more real healthcare resources), an education deficit (retire all student debt), an infrastructure deficit (fix it), an inequality defi-cit (taxes and redistribution). Clearly, Kelton advocates replacing Adam Smith's invisible hand with Uncle Sam's hugely visible one.

As we see it, one of the major flaws of MMT is that excessive spending that causes inflation would have to be offset with higher taxes for the private sector. Kelton herself admits that if the government wants to boost spending in a targeted area, it may "need to remove some spending power from the rest of us to prevent its own more generous outlays from pushing up prices." One way to create this room is through higher taxes. Taxes are also a "powerful way for governments to alter the distribution of wealth and income." Governments can also use taxes "to encourage or discourage certain behaviors."[136]

"Capitalist economies chronically operate" without "enough combined spending (public and private) to induce companies to offer employment for every person who wants to work," Kelton writes.[137] She adds: "There isn't a capitalist economy on earth that has found a way to eradicate the business cycle."[138] Kelton argues that MMT could be used to get the economy to full employment and smooth the business cycle.

Kelton envisions a "universal right of employment" whereby a "Public Service Employment (PSE) program" would offer "paid work at a living wage" of $15 per hour "with a basic package of benefits that include health care and paid leave."[139] "Think of it" as binders on a shelf "filled with a wide variety of available jobs." Enough jobs to "allow people with different skills and interests to walk in without a job and walk out with one that fits them." The program would be focused on utilizing workers to build a "care economy" oriented around our aging society.

This remarkably ambitious program would automatically stabilize fiscal spending to where it needs to be to balance full employment with stable inflation. When the economy hits a recession (or recovers), the PSE program ramps up (or down). This raises some obvious questions. If people are content with their government job, why would they leave? What about workers who say they want to work but are routinely absent? How do you address structural problems like mismatches between the government's skill needs in a particular region and their availability in the local job market?

Kelton's book leaves no doubt about what MMT is all about: It's an agenda for more big government and higher taxes. Kelton's views must strike many conservatives as unrealistic and utopian. Proponents of free market capitalism might exclaim: "Pay no attention to the professor behind the curtain!"

For now, the central banks continue to pour liquidity into global financial markets. Fiscal policymakers have joined the stimulus party, resulting in the global implementation of MMT, i.e., massive fiscal deficits financed by massive quantitative easing.

Kelton has won the debate, for now, on the heels of the GVC. Nevertheless, recall that *The Wizard of Oz* was all about a bad dream Dorothy had after getting hit on the head.

TINA Plus MMT

A trillion here, a trillion there adds up to serious money. In MMT's dreamland, taken to the extreme, government deficits are bottomless pits. If they can be financed so easily with easy money without boosting inflation, why do we bother collecting taxes? We would be big advocates of MMT if our taxes were cut to zero. Let's give it a try! Why not? Anything is possible in Oz.

While MMT hasn't boosted inflation, as measured by consumer prices, so far, it certainly has boosted asset inflation, potentially fueling the Mother of All Meltups (MAMU), which potentially could set the stage for the Mother of All Meltdowns (MAMD). In recent years, many stock market bulls have argued that "there is no alternative" to stocks because bond yields have been so low. TINA (There Is No Alternative) made even more sense after the

Fed and the Treasury embraced MMT at the end of March 2020. The stock market equation from March 23—at least through this writing in January 2021—has been TINA + MMT = MAMU.

Epilogue

Wish Comes True

Professor Kelton proclaims that to see through the "deficit myth," all we need to do is click our heels three times. With the power of Modern Monetary Theory, we can give birth to the "people's economy."

The pandemic ripped our economy from its foundation, causing us to crash-land in MMT's dreamworld. So here we are with no limits on Treasury budget deficits or on Fed purchases of Treasury securities. The sky is the limit for T-Fed in MMT land.

Kelton isn't the only MMT wizard in Oz. Joining her are the wizards at the major central banks. We should all continue to pay close attention to these men and women behind the monetary curtains. In response to the pandemic, they flooded Oz with liquidity during 2020. They were on course to continue doing so as 2021 began.

For investors, unlimited MMT has led to a dreamworld for valuation, especially for cryptocurrencies. The yellow brick road is paved with bitcoins, which soared 305% during 2020 from $7,180 to $29,112. There's no way to value the cryptocurrency since it doesn't generate earnings, distribute dividends, yield coupons, or pay rent. It is similar to gold in that respect. In addition, the supply of bitcoins—like the supply of gold—is limited and can't be manipulated by central banks (unless they start conducting open-market operations in the cryptocurrency). Nevertheless, the ratio of the price of bitcoin to the spot price of gold has been just as volatile as the price of the digital currency.

The ratio of the price of bitcoin to the S&P 500 stock price index has also been volatile. The former's increase of 305% during 2020 far outpaced the 16.3% increase in the S&P 500. Valuation metrics for the S&P 500 all rose to either record or near record levels at the end of 2020. They could be justified by record-low bond yields. However, the 10-year US Treasury bond yield was trending higher during 2020 after falling to a record low during August.

Fed Chair Jerome Powell is the most important wizard in Oz. That's because unlike the movie's wizard, he really is great and powerful, or at least he was in 2020 when the Fed successfully won the battles on the financial and economic fronts of the world war against the virus. Again, our conclusion is: Don't fight the Fed, especially when it is fighting a pandemic!

At the start of 2021, just before we went to press, Powell reiterated that the Fed isn't even thinking about thinking about exiting Oz. He spoke on Thursday, January 14 in a virtual chat hosted by the Princeton University Bendheim Center for Finance. He affirmed his commitment to keeping interest rates low for the foreseeable future, even though he said that the economic recovery has been better than expected. More specifically, he said: "When the time comes to raise interest rates, we'll certainly do that, and that time, by the way, is no time soon."

Powell also remarked during his virtual chat that real economic activity has made a surprisingly rapid recovery and said that he is optimistic about the outlook: "[W]e could be back to the old economic peak fairly soon and passing it. We may bypass a lot of the damage that we were concerned about to low- and moderate-income people."[140]

Meanwhile, Powell's wish for more fiscal stimulus to combat the pandemic came true the very same day of his virtual chat.

In a speech Thursday evening, President-elect Joe Biden called for a $1.9 trillion American Rescue Plan, including a round of $1,400-per-person direct payments to most households to supplement the $600 checks sent in January 2021, a $400-a-week unemployment insurance supplement through September, expanded paid leave, and increases in the child tax credit. Aid for households makes up about half of the plan's cost, with much of the rest going to vaccine distribution and state and local governments.

On January 14, *The Wall Street Journal* reported: "The president-elect won't offer spending-cut or tax-increase offsets for his plan and will instead rely on federal borrowing, according to a Biden official."[141] Our guess is that Treasury Secretary Janet Yellen might have been the unnamed source. She knew that the Fed publicly committed to purchasing $80 billion per month in US Treasury securities. Odds are that she already received assurances from Powell that the Fed would buy more if necessary. That's what MMT-BFFs (best friends forever) at T-Fed do for one another.

On Friday, January 15, Boston Federal Reserve President Eric Rosengren became the first Fed official to publicly speak on Biden's plan. "It's a big package, but I think it's appropriate," he told CNBC's Steve Liesman during an interview. "And to the extent that it targets those parts of the economy most affected by the pandemic, that is the appropriate action for fiscal policy at this time."[142]

It all adds up to Modern Monetary Theory on speed and steroids.

Forward Guidance

One final point on the Fed's latest "forward guidance," i.e., as of this writing in January 2021.

In my book *Fed Watching*, I observed that the Fed chairs and their colleagues have tended to communicate their policy intentions by repeating certain keywords, like "gradual," "patient," and "appropriate." The goal of this word game is to come up with one word or a short phrase that best describes and communicates both the current stance and the future course of monetary policy. That word or phrase then is used repeatedly in the Fed's written releases, such as the FOMC statements and minutes, as well as verbally in the speeches and interviews of the Fed chair and other Fed officials. It becomes their monetary policy mantra.

The phrase "substantial further progress" could be the Fed's latest mantra. It first appeared in the December 16, 2020 FOMC statement: "In addition, the Federal Reserve will continue to increase its holdings of Treasury securities by at least $80 billion per month and of agency mortgage-backed securities by at least $40 billion per month until substantial further progress has been made toward the Committee's maximum employment and price stability goals."[143]

The rub was that the latest round of stimulus increased the odds that substantial further progress on the economic and inflation fronts would be made sooner rather than later in 2021 and 2022. If so, then Powell might have to reconsider his "no time soon" pledge about tightening monetary policy sooner rather than later.

Acknowledgments

Our colleagues at Yardeni Research deserve a great deal of credit for helping us to put this study together. Debbie Johnson and Mali Quintana spent countless hours checking the data that are shown in the book's text and charts. Jackie Doherty provided numerous good editorial suggestions. Mary Fanslau helped to administer the project. Geoff Moore and Steve Rybka delivered great tech support.

Our in-house editor, Sandra Cohan, cheerfully and masterfully pulled double duty by editing the book and our daily commentary. Her dedication to making the book happen was impressive.

Tom Clemmons also provided great editorial support. David Wogahn skillfully coordinated the production of the book.

Collectively, they provided many improvements; we take full responsibility for any remaining errors and omissions.

Appendices

1. FOMC Summary of Economic Projections
   https://www.yardenibook.com/pub/fedgvc-appendix1.pdf

2. A Timeline of the Covid-19 Pandemic, 2020
   https://www.yardenibook.com/pub/fedgvc-appendix2.pdf

3. The Fed's Liquidity Facilities, 2020
   https://www.yardenibook.com/pub/fedgvc-appendix3.pdf

4. The Phases of Clinical Trials
   https://www.yardenibook.com/pub/fedgvc-appendix4.pdf

Acronyms and Abbreviations

ABS .... asset-backed securities
AGI .... adjusted gross income
AIT .... Average Inflation Targeting
APP .... Asset Purchase Programme
BEA .... Bureau of Economic Analysis
BLS .... Bureau of Labor Statistics
BOC .... Bank of Canada
BOJ .... Bank of Japan
CARES ..... Coronavirus Aid, Relief, and Economic Security
CBO .... Congressional Budget Office
CDC .... Centers for Disease Control
CECL .... current expected credit loss
CEI .... Coincident Economic Indicators
CPFF .... Commercial Paper Funding Facility
CPI .... Consumer Price Index
CSPP .... Corporate Sector Purchase Programme
D .... Democrat
EC .... European Commission
ECB .... European Central Bank
EEC .... European Economic Community
EMU .... European Monetary Union
ESF .... Exchange Stabilization Fund
ESI........... Economic Sentiment Indicator
ETF .... exchange-traded fund
EU .... European Union
EUA .... Emergency Use Authorization
FAIT .... Flexible Average Inflation Targeting
FAITH...... Flexible Average Inflation Targeting Hope

FIMA .... Foreign and International Monetary Authorities
FOMC ...... Federal Open Market Committee
FRB .... Federal Reserve Board
FSR .... Financial Stability Report
GDP .... gross domestic product
GFC .... Great Financial Crisis
GFSR .... Global Financial Stability Report
GNP .... gross national product
GVC .... Great Virus Crisis
IMF .... International Monetary Fund
ISM .... Institute for Supply Management
J-REIT ...... Japanese Real Estate Investment Trust
LTRO .... Longer-Term Refinancing Operation
MAMU .... Mother of All Melt-Ups
MBS .... mortgage-backed security
MLF .... Municipal Liquidity Facility
MAMD .... Mother of All Meltdowns
MMLF ..... Money Market Mutual Fund Liquidity Facility
MMT .... Modern Monetary Theory
MPR .... Monetary Policy Report
MSLP .... Main Street Lending Program
NAIRU .... non-accelerating inflation rate of unemployment
NBER .... National Bureau of Economic Research
NGEU ...... Next Generation EU
NIPA .... National Income and Product Accounts
NIRP .... negative-interest-rate policies
NSA .... not seasonally adjusted
PAYGO .... Pay As You Go
PCE .... personal consumption expenditures
PCED .... personal consumption expenditures deflator
PDCF .... Primary Dealer Credit Facility
PELTRO .. Pandemic Emergency Longer-Term Refinancing Operations
PEPP .... Pandemic Emergency Purchase Programme
PMCCF .... Primary Market Corporate Credit Facility
PMI .... Purchasing Managers' Index

PPI .... Producer Price Index

PPP .... Paycheck Protection Program

PPPLF...... Paycheck Protection Program Liquidity Facility

PPT .... Plunge Protection Team

PSE........... Public Service Employment

QE .... quantitative easing

QQE......... qualitative and quantitative easing

QT............ quantitative tightening

R................ Republican

S&P.......... Standard & Poor's

SA............. seasonally adjusted

SBA .... Small Business Administration

SEC .... Securities and Exchange Commission

SAAR....... Seasonally Adjusted Annual Rate

SEP........... Summary of Economic Projections

SMCCF ... Secondary Market Corporate Credit Facility

SME .... small and medium enterprise

SPV .... special purpose vehicle

SURE .... Support to mitigate Unemployment Risks in an Emergency

TALF....... Term Asset-Backed Securities Loan Facility

TARP .... Troubled Asset Relief Program

TINA........ there is no alternative

TLTRO..... Targeted Longer-Term Refinancing Operations

WEI.......... Weekly Economic Index

WHO .... World Health Organization

WTO .... World Trade Organization

WWV....... world war against the virus

YCT.......... yield-curve targeting

YRI........... Yardeni Research, Inc.

ZIRP......... zero-interest-rate policies

Author's Note

This study is another in a series of Topical Studies examining issues that I discussed in my book *Predicting the Markets: A Professional Autobiography* (2018) but in greater detail and on a more current basis. Previous studies in this series, which are available on my Amazon homepage, include:

S&P 500 Earnings, Valuation, and the Pandemic (2020)

Fed Watching for Fun and Profit (2020)

Stock Buybacks: The True Story (2019)

The Yield Curve: What Is It Really Predicting? (2019)

The charts at the end of this study were current as of January 23, 2021. They are available in color along with linked endnotes and appendices at **www.yardenibook.com/studies**.

Institutional investors are invited to sign up for the Yardeni Research service on a complimentary trial basis at **www.yardeni.com/trial-registration**.

Figures

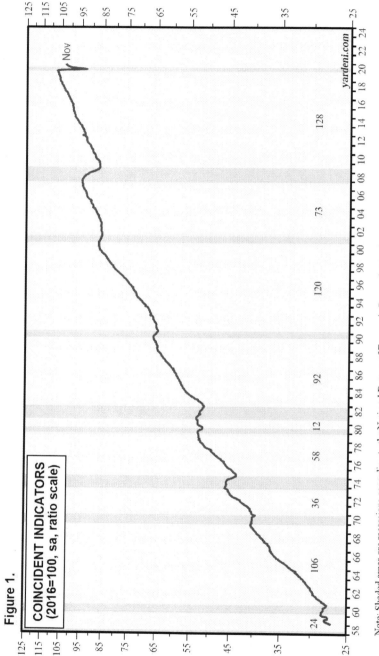

Figure 1.

COINCIDENT INDICATORS
(2016=100, sa, ratio scale)

Note: Shaded areas are recessions according to the National Bureau of Economic Research. Numbers above time line reflect number of months of expansion.
Source: Bureau of Economic Analysis.

yardeni.com

Figure 2.

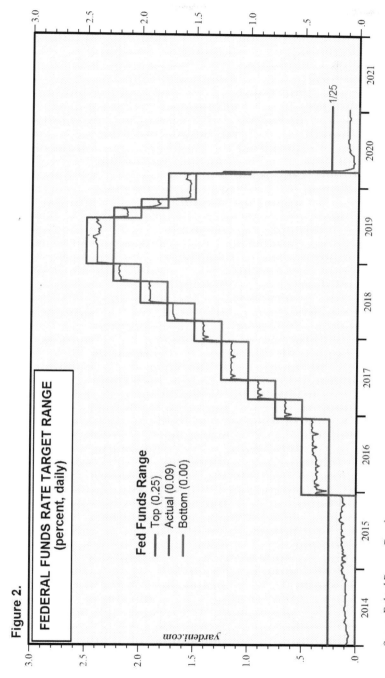

FEDERAL FUNDS RATE TARGET RANGE
(percent, daily)

Fed Funds Range
Top (0.25)
Actual (0.09)
Bottom (0.00)

Source: Federal Reserve Board.

Figure 3.

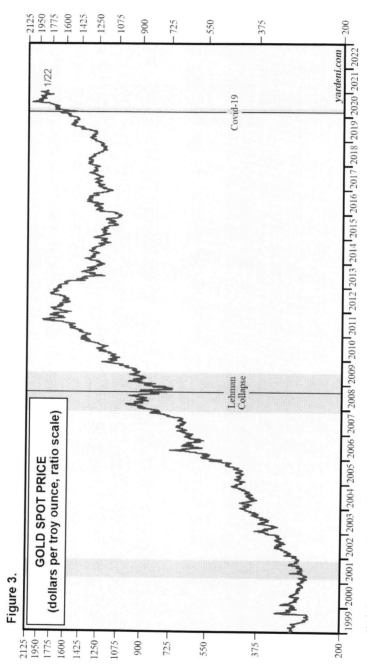

GOLD SPOT PRICE
(dollars per troy ounce, ratio scale)

Shaded areas are recessions according to the National Bureau of Economic Research.
Note: Lehman collapsed 9/15/2008. WHO declared global Covid-19 pandemic on 3/11/2020.
Source: Wall Street Journal and Haver Analytics.

Figure 4.

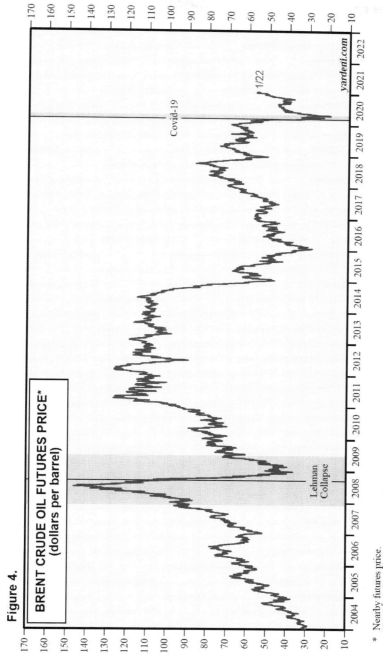

BRENT CRUDE OIL FUTURES PRICE*
(dollars per barrel)

* Nearby futures price.
Shaded areas are recessions according to the National Bureau of Economic Research.
Note: Lehman collapsed 9/15/2008. WHO declared global Covid-19 pandemic on 3/11/2020.
Source: Haver Analytics.

yardeni.com

Figure 5.

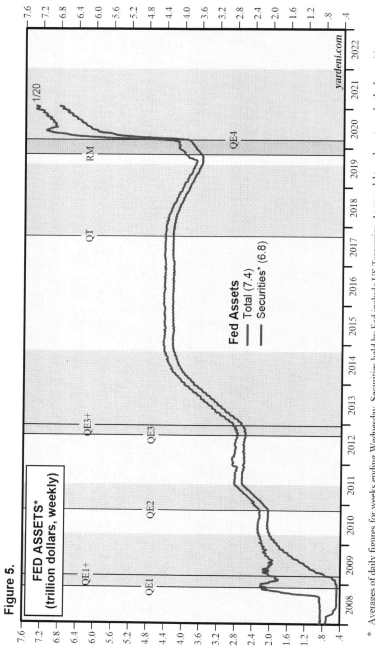

FED ASSETS*
(trillion dollars, weekly)

Fed Assets
— Total (7.4)
— Securities* (6.8)

yardeni.com

* Averages of daily figures for weeks ending Wednesday. Securities held by Fed include US Treasuries, Agency debt, and mortgage-backed securities.
  Note: QE1 (11/25/08-3/31/10) = $1.24tn in mortgage securities; expanded (3/16/09-3/31/10) = $300bn in Treasuries. QE2 (11/3/10-6/30/11) = $600bn
  in Treasuries. QE3 (9/13/12-10/29/14) = $40bn/month in mortgage securities (open ended); expanded (12/12/12-10/1/14) = $45bn/month in Treasuries.
  QT (10/1/17-7/31/19) = balance sheet pared by $675bn. RM (11/1/19-3/15/20) = reserve management. $60bn/month in Treasury bills. QE4 (3/16/20-infinity).
  Source: Federal Reserve Board.

Figure 6.

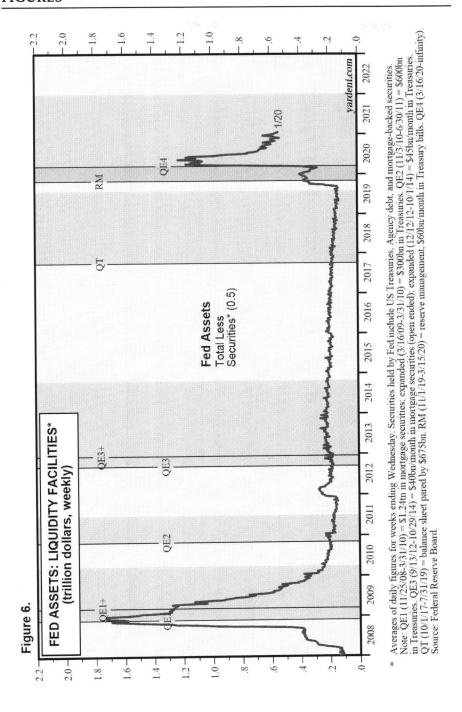

* Averages of daily figures for weeks ending Wednesday. Securities held by Fed include US Treasuries, Agency debt, and mortgage-backed securities.
Note: QE1 (11/25/08-3/31/10) = $1.24tn in mortgage securities: expanded (3/16/09-3/31/10) = $300bn in Treasuries. QE2 (11/3/10-6/30/11) = $600bn
in Treasuries. QE3 (9/13/12-10/29/14) = $40bn/month in mortgage securities (open ended): expanded (12/12/12-10/1/14) = $45bn/month in Treasuries.
QT (10/1/17-7/31/19) = balance sheet pared by $675bn. RM (11/1/19-3/15/20) = reserve management. $60bn/month in Treasury bills. QE4 (3/16/20-infinity).
Source: Federal Reserve Board.

Figure 7.

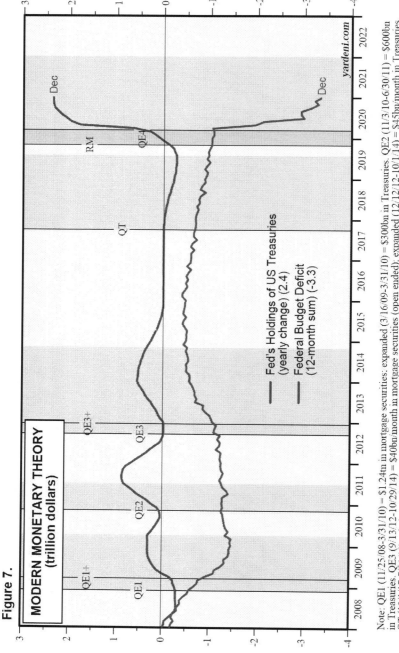

MODERN MONETARY THEORY
(trillion dollars)

Fed's Holdings of US Treasuries
(yearly change) (2.4)

Federal Budget Deficit
(12-month sum) (-3.3)

yardeni.com

Note: QE1 (11/25/08-3/31/10) = $1.24tn in mortgage securities: expanded (3/16/09-3/31/10) = $300bn in Treasuries. QE2 (11/3/10-6/30/11) = $600bn in Treasuries. QE3 (9/13/12-10/29/14) = $40bn/month in mortgage securities (open ended): expanded (12/12/12-10/1/14) = $45bn/month in Treasuries. QT (10/1/17-7/31/19) = balance sheet pared by $675bn. RM (11/1/19-3/15/20) = reserve management. $60bn/month in Treasury bills. QE4 (3/16/20-infinity). Source: Federal Reserve Board and US Treasury Department.

Figure 8.

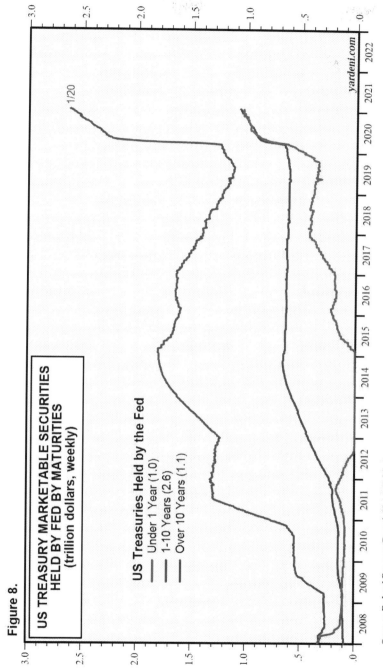

US TREASURY MARKETABLE SECURITIES
HELD BY FED BY MATURITIES
(trillion dollars, weekly)

US Treasuries Held by the Fed
— Under 1 Year (1.0)
— 1-10 Years (2.6)
— Over 10 Years (1.1)

1/20

yardeni.com

Source: Federal Reserve Board. H.4.1 Table 2.

Figure 9.

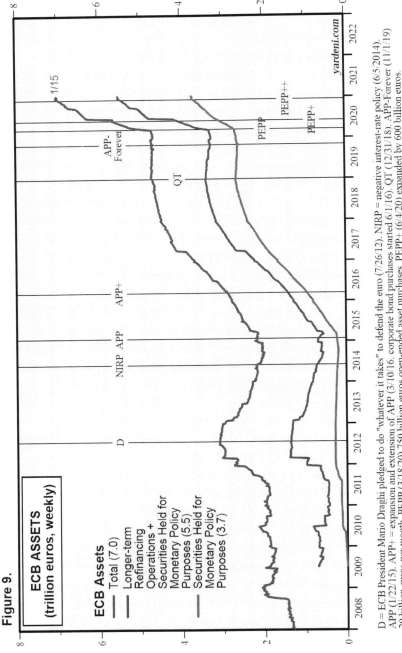

D = ECB President Mario Draghi pledged to do "whatever it takes" to defend the euro (7/26/12). NIRP = negative interest-rate policy (6/5/2014). APP (1/22/15). APP+ = expansion and extension of APP (3/10/16, corporate bond purchases started 6/1/16). QT (12/31/18). APP-Forever (11/1/19). 20 billion euros per month. PEPP (3/18/20) 750 billion euros open-ended asset purchases. PEPP+ (6/4/20) expanded by 600 billion euros. PEPP++ (12/10/20) another 500 billion euros in purchases.
Source: European Central Bank.

Figure 10.

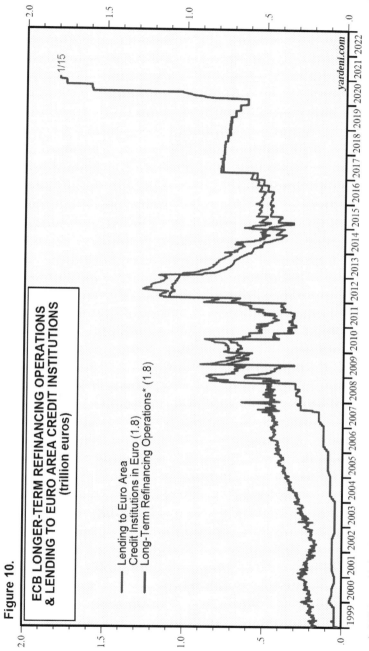

ECB LONGER-TERM REFINANCING OPERATIONS
& LENDING TO EURO AREA CREDIT INSTITUTIONS
(trillion euros)

Lending to Euro Area
Credit Institutions in Euro (1.8)
Long-Term Refinancing Operations* (1.8)

* LTROs provide low interest-rate funding to Eurozone banks with sovereign debt as collateral on the loans. The loans are offered monthly by the ECB and
are typically repaid in three months, six months, or one year.
Source: European Central Bank.

yardeni.com

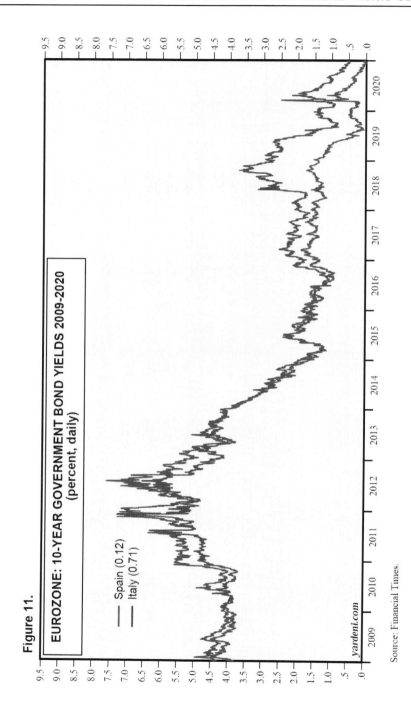

Figure 11.

EUROZONE: 10-YEAR GOVERNMENT BOND YIELDS 2009-2020
(percent, daily)

Spain (0.12)
Italy (0.71)

yardeni.com

Source: Financial Times.

Figure 12.

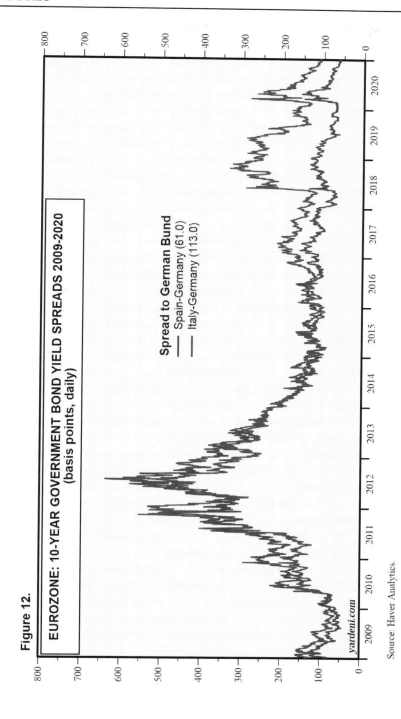

EUROZONE: 10-YEAR GOVERNMENT BOND YIELD SPREADS 2009-2020
(basis points, daily)

Spread to German Bund
Spain-Germany (61.0)
Italy-Germany (113.0)

yardeni.com

Source: Haver Analytics.

Figure 13.

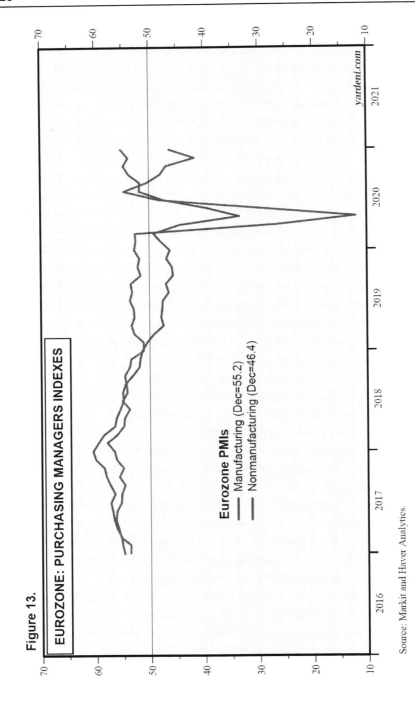

EUROZONE: PURCHASING MANAGERS INDEXES

Eurozone PMIs
Manufacturing (Dec=55.2)
Nonmanufacturing (Dec=46.4)

Source: Markit and Haver Analytics.

Figure 14.

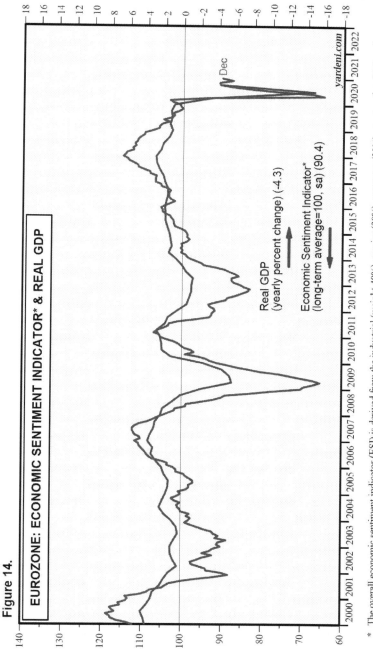

EUROZONE: ECONOMIC SENTIMENT INDICATOR* & REAL GDP

Real GDP
(yearly percent change) (-4.3)

Economic Sentiment Indicator*
(long-term average=100, sa) (90.4)

Dec

yardeni.com

* The overall economic sentiment indicator (ESI) is derived from the industrial (weight 40%), service (30%), consumer (20%), construction (5%), and retail trade (5%) confidence indicators.
Source: Statistical Office of the European Communities, European Commission, and Haver Analytics.

Figure 15.

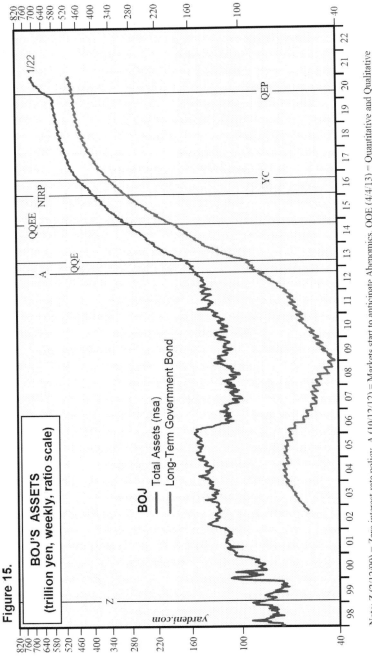

**BOJ'S ASSETS
(trillion yen, weekly, ratio scale)**

BOJ
— Total Assets (nsa)
— Long-Term Government Bond

Note: Z (2/12/99) = Zero interest-rate policy. A (10/12/12) = Markets start to anticipate Abenomics. QQE (4/4/13) = Quantitative and Qualitative Easing. QQEE (10/31/14) = expanded and extended version of QQE. NIRP (1/29/16) = Negative interest-rate policy. YC (9/21/16) = Yield curve targeting. QEP (4/27/20) = Unlimited QE during pandemic.
Source: Bank of Japan.

Figure 16.

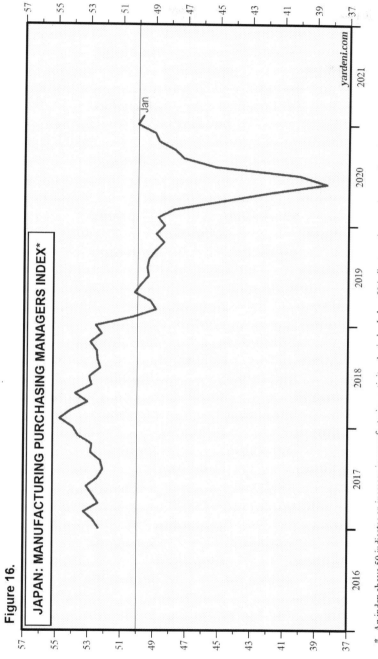

JAPAN: MANUFACTURING PURCHASING MANAGERS INDEX*

yardeni.com

* An index above 50 indicates an increase in manufacturing activity. An index below 50 indicates a decrease in manufacturing activity.
  Source: Markit and Haver Analytics.

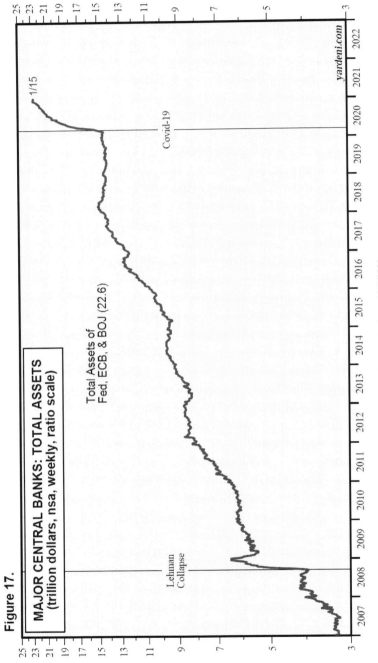

Figure 17.

MAJOR CENTRAL BANKS: TOTAL ASSETS
(trillion dollars, nsa, weekly, ratio scale)

Total Assets of
Fed, ECB, & BOJ (22.6)

Lehman
Collapse

Covid-19

1/15

yardeni.com

Note: Lehman collapsed 9/15/2008. WHO declared global Covid-19 pandemic on 3/11/2020.
Source: Haver Analytics.

Figure 18.

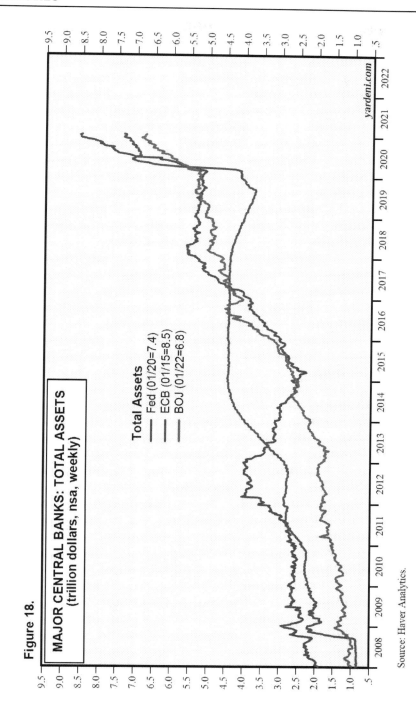

MAJOR CENTRAL BANKS: TOTAL ASSETS
(trillion dollars, nsa, weekly)

Total Assets
Fed (01/20=7.4)
ECB (01/15=8.5)
BOJ (01/22=6.8)

Source: Haver Analytics.

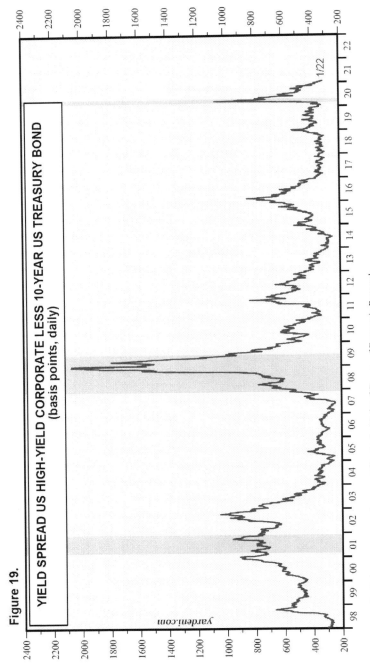

Figure 19.

YIELD SPREAD US HIGH-YIELD CORPORATE LESS 10-YEAR US TREASURY BOND
(basis points, daily)

Note: Shaded areas are recessions according to the National Bureau of Economic Research.
Source: Bank of America Merrill Lynch and Federal Reserve Board.

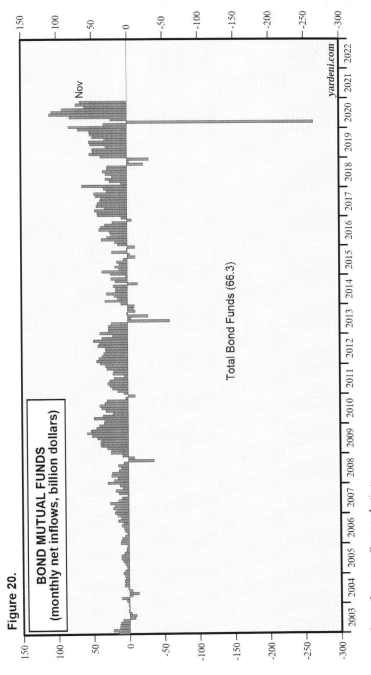

Figure 20.

BOND MUTUAL FUNDS
(monthly net inflows, billion dollars)

Total Bond Funds (66.3)

Nov

yardeni.com

Source: Investment Company Institute.

Figure 21.

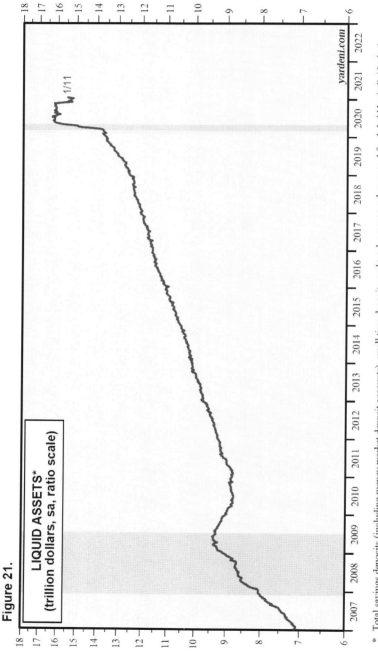

LIQUID ASSETS*
(trillion dollars, sa, ratio scale)

yardeni.com

* Total savings deposits (including money market deposit accounts), small time deposits, and total money market mutual funds held by individuals & institutions.
Note: Shaded areas are recessions according to the National Bureau of Economic Research.
Source: Federal Reserve Board.

Figure 22.

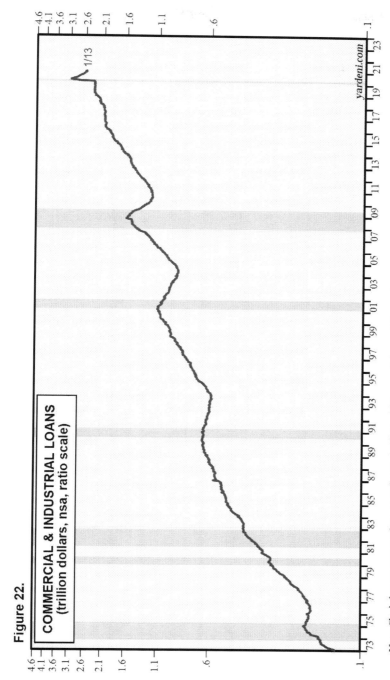

COMMERCIAL & INDUSTRIAL LOANS
(trillion dollars, nsa, ratio scale)

Note: Shaded areas are recessions according to the National Bureau of Economic Research.
Source: Federal Reserve Board.

yardeni.com

Figure 23.

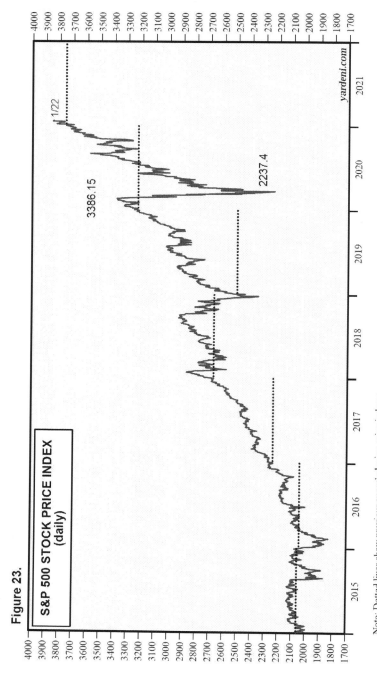

S&P 500 STOCK PRICE INDEX
(daily)

Note: Dotted lines show previous years' closing price indexes.
Source: Standard & Poor's.

Figure 24.

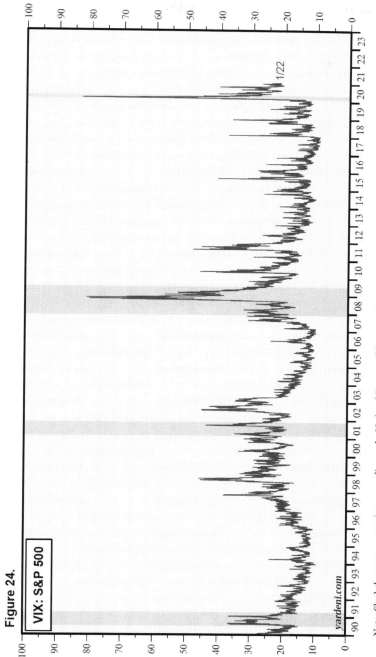

VIX: S&P 500

yardeni.com

Note: Shaded areas are recessions according to the National Bureau of Economic Research.
Source: Chicago Board Options Exchange.

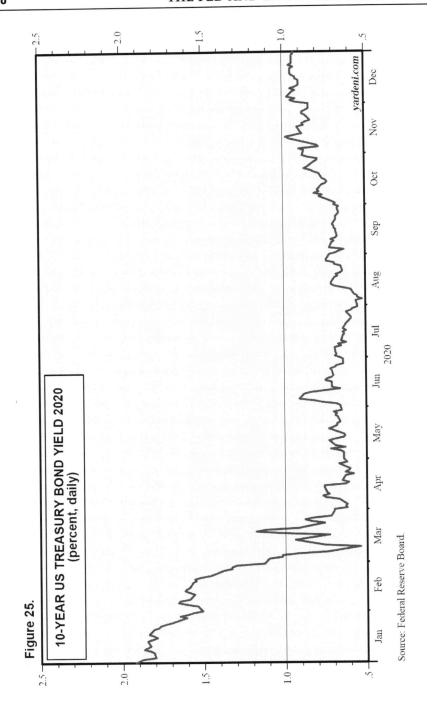

Figure 25.

10-YEAR US TREASURY BOND YIELD 2020
(percent, daily)

Source: Federal Reserve Board.

Figure 26.

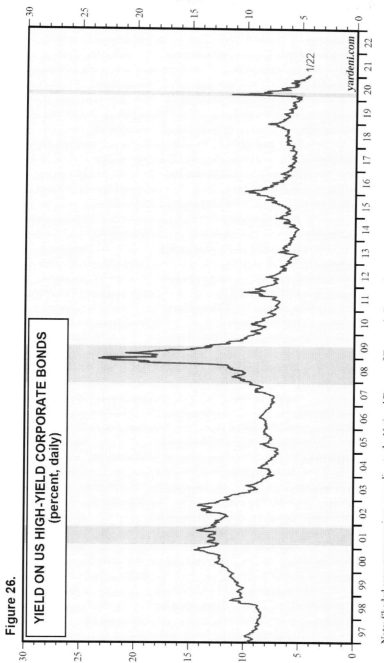

YIELD ON US HIGH-YIELD CORPORATE BONDS
(percent, daily)

1/22

yardeni.com

Note: Shaded areas are recessions according to the National Bureau of Economic Research.
Source: Bank of America Merrill Lynch.

Figure 27.

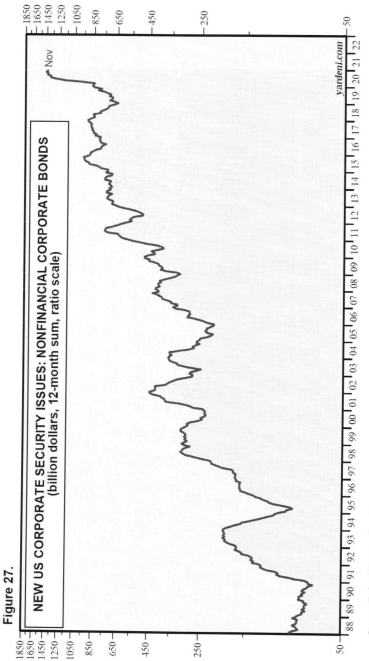

NEW US CORPORATE SECURITY ISSUES: NONFINANCIAL CORPORATE BONDS
(billion dollars, 12-month sum, ratio scale)

Source: Federal Reserve Board.

Figure 28.

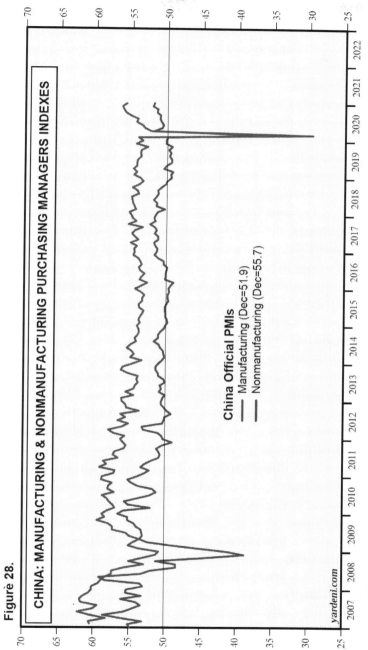

CHINA: MANUFACTURING & NONMANUFACTURING PURCHASING MANAGERS INDEXES

China Official PMIs
— Manufacturing (Dec=51.9)
— Nonmanufacturing (Dec=55.7)

yardeni.com

Source: China Federation Logistics & Purchasing and Haver Analytics.

Figure 29.

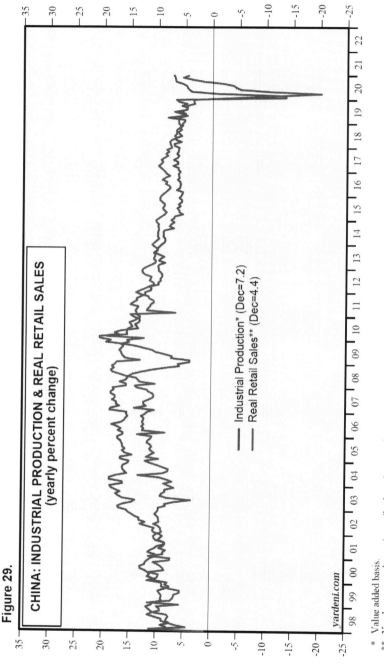

CHINA: INDUSTRIAL PRODUCTION & REAL RETAIL SALES
(yearly percent change)

Industrial Production* (Dec=7.2)
Real Retail Sales** (Dec=4.4)

yardeni.com

* Value added basis.
** Yearly percent change in retail sales minus yearly percent change in CPI.
Source: China National Bureau of Statistics.

Figure 30.

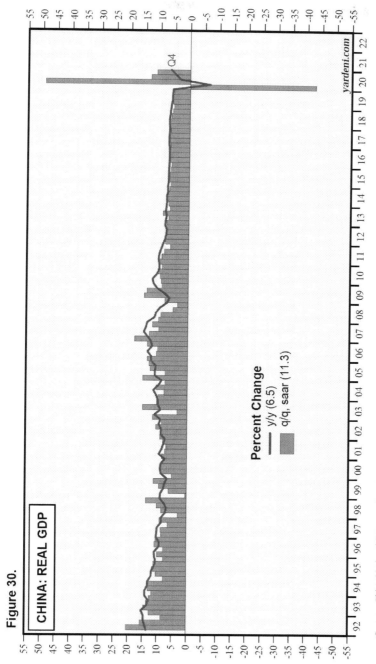

CHINA: REAL GDP

Percent Change
— y/y (6.5)
▬ q/q, saar (11.3)

Q4

Source: China National Bureau of Statistics and Haver Analytics.

yardeni.com

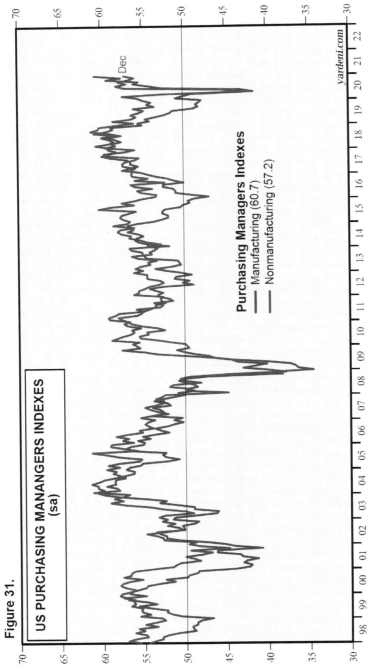

Figure 31.

US PURCHASING MANANGERS INDEXES
(sa)

Purchasing Managers Indexes
Manufacturing (60.7)
Nonmanufacturing (57.2)

Source: Institute of Supply Management.

Figure 32.

RETAIL SALES
(trillion dollars, saar)

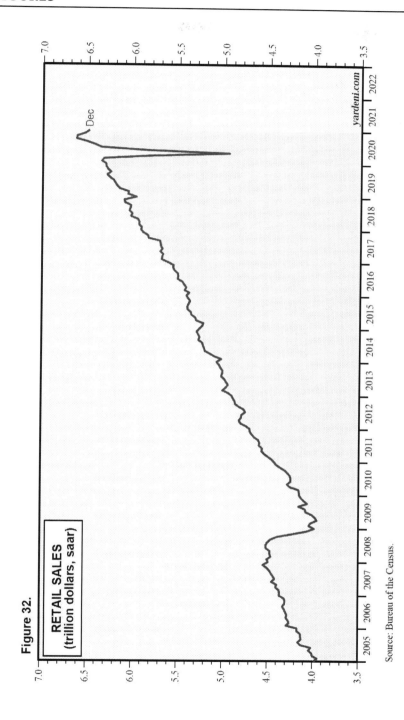

Source: Bureau of the Census.

Figure 33.

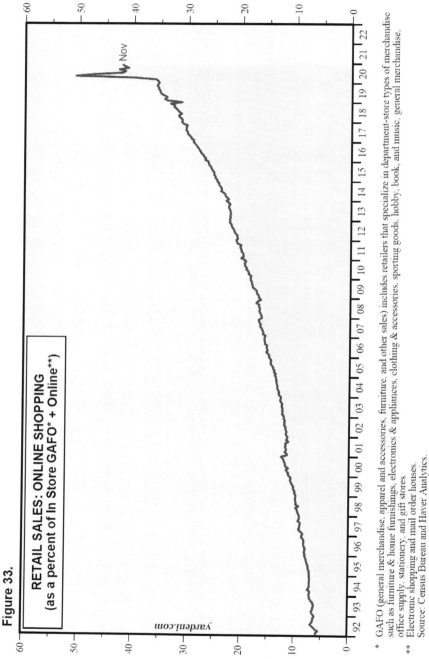

RETAIL SALES: ONLINE SHOPPING
(as a percent of In Store GAFO* + Online**)

* GAFO (general merchandise, apparel and accessories, furniture, and other sales) includes retailers that specialize in department-store types of merchandise such as furniture & home furnishings, electronics & appliances, clothing & accessories, sporting goods, hobby, book, and music, general merchandise, office supply, stationery, and gift stores.
** Electronic shopping and mail order houses.
Source: Census Bureau and Haver Analytics.

Figure 34.

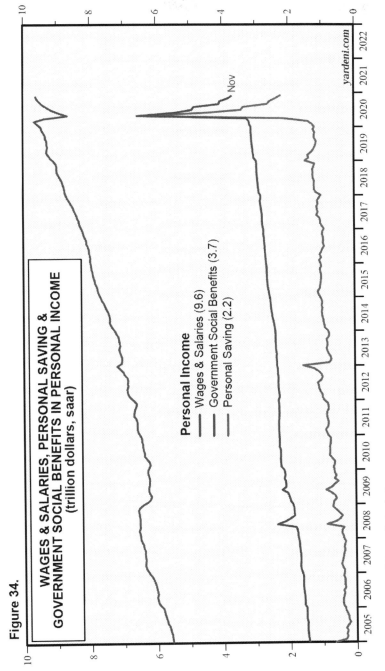

**WAGES & SALARIES, PERSONAL SAVING &
GOVERNMENT SOCIAL BENEFITS IN PERSONAL INCOME**
(trillion dollars, saar)

Personal Income
—— Wages & Salaries (9.6)
—— Government Social Benefits (3.7)
—— Personal Saving (2.2)

Nov

yardeni.com

Source: Bureau of Economic Analysis.

Figure 35.

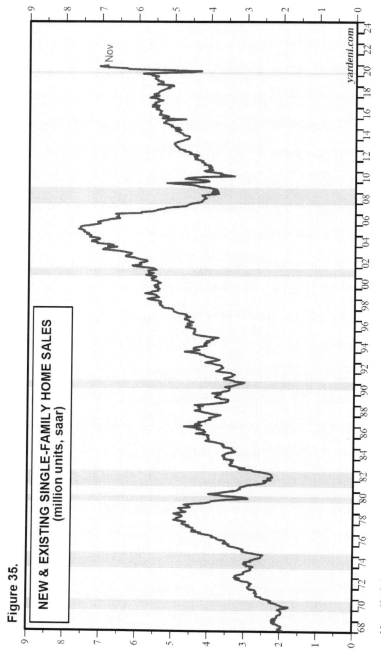

NEW & EXISTING SINGLE-FAMILY HOME SALES
(million units, saar)

Note: Shaded areas are recessions according to the National Bureau of Economic Research.
Source: Census Bureau and National Association of Realtors.

yardeni.com

Figure 36.

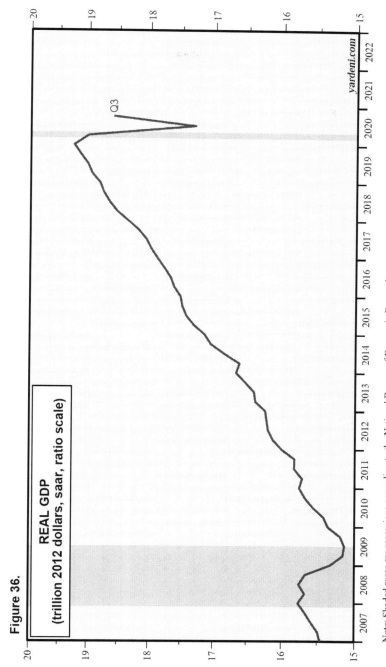

REAL GDP
(trillion 2012 dollars, saar, ratio scale)

Q3

Note: Shaded areas are recessions according to the National Bureau of Economic Research.
Source: Bureau of Economic Analysis.

yardeni.com

Figure 37.

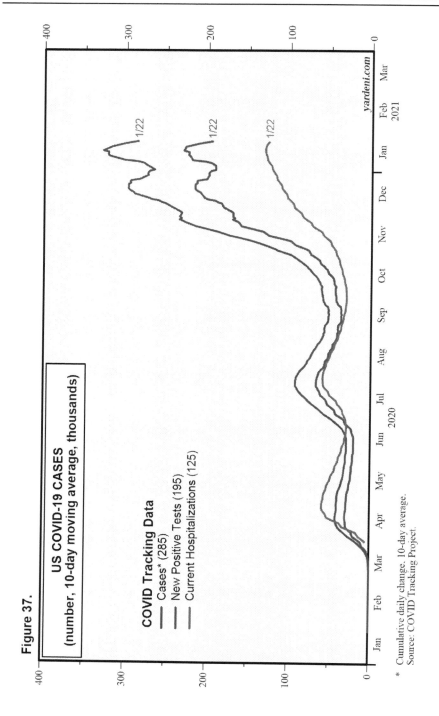

US COVID-19 CASES
(number, 10-day moving average, thousands)

COVID Tracking Data
— Cases* (285)
— New Positive Tests (195)
— Current Hospitalizations (125)

* Cumulative daily change. 10-day average.
Source: COVID Tracking Project.

yardeni.com

Figure 38.

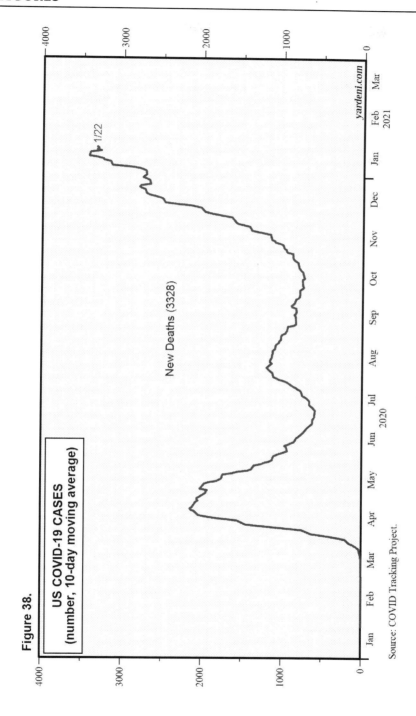

US COVID-19 CASES
(number, 10-day moving average)

New Deaths (3328)

1/22

Source: COVID Tracking Project.

yardeni.com

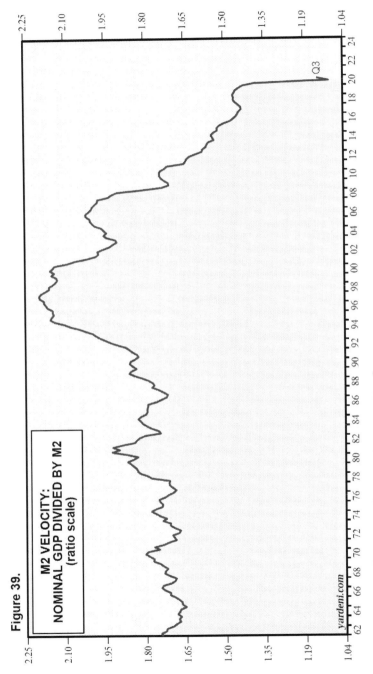

Figure 39.

M2 VELOCITY:
NOMINAL GDP DIVIDED BY M2
(ratio scale)

Source: Bureau of Economic Analysis and Federal Reserve Board.

Figure 40.

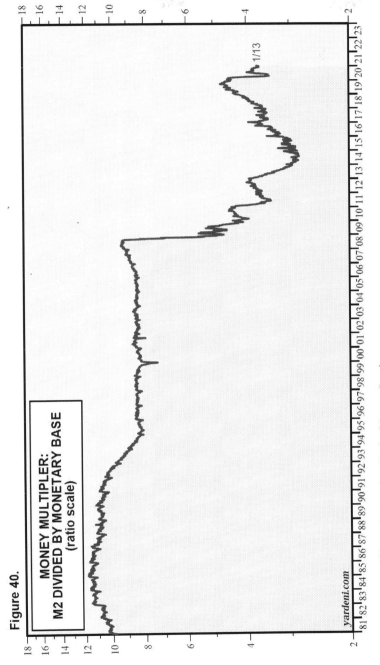

MONEY MULTIPLER:
M2 DIVIDED BY MONETARY BASE
(ratio scale)

1/13

yardeni.com

Source: Bureau of Economic Analysis and Federal Reserve Board.

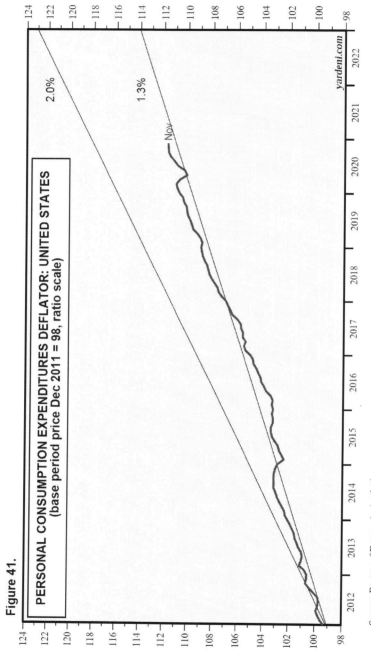

Figure 41.

PERSONAL CONSUMPTION EXPENDITURES DEFLATOR: UNITED STATES
(base period price Dec 2011 = 98, ratio scale)

Source: Bureau of Economic Analysis.

Figure 42.

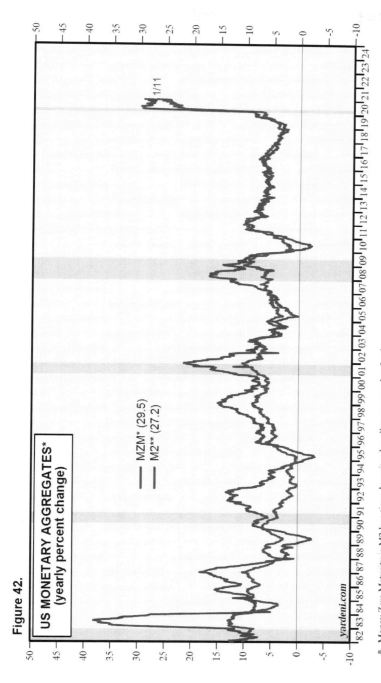

US MONETARY AGGREGATES*
(yearly percent change)

—— MZM* (29.5)
—— M2** (27.2)

1/11

yardeni.com

* Money Zero Maturity is M2 less time deposits plus all money market funds.
** M2 is M1 plus most savings accounts. money market accounts. retail money market mutual funds. and small denomination time deposits (certificates of deposit of under $100,000).
Note: Shaded areas are recessions according to the National Bureau of Economic Research.
Source: Federal Reserve Board.

Figure 43.

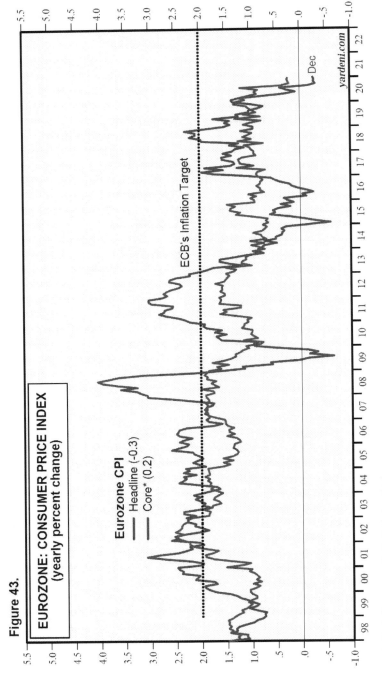

EUROZONE: CONSUMER PRICE INDEX
(yearly percent change)

Eurozone CPI
— Headline (-0.3)
— Core* (0.2)

ECB's Inflation Target

Dec

yardeni.com

* Excluding energy, food, alcohol, and tobacco.
Source: Statistical Office of the European Communities.

Figure 44.

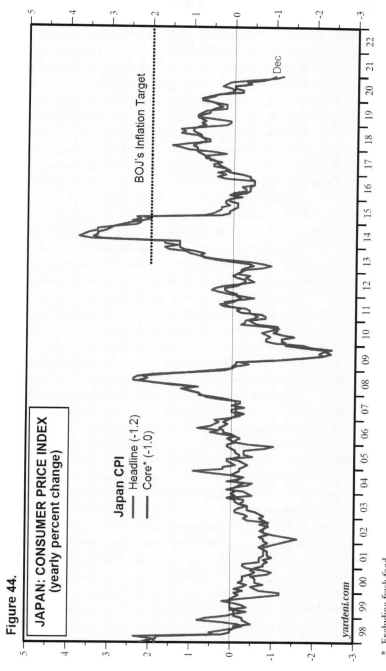

JAPAN: CONSUMER PRICE INDEX
(yearly percent change)

Japan CPI
— Headline (-1.2)
— Core* (-1.0)

BOJ's Inflation Target

Dec

yardeni.com

* Excluding fresh food.
Source: Ministry of Internal Affairs and Communications.

Figure 45.

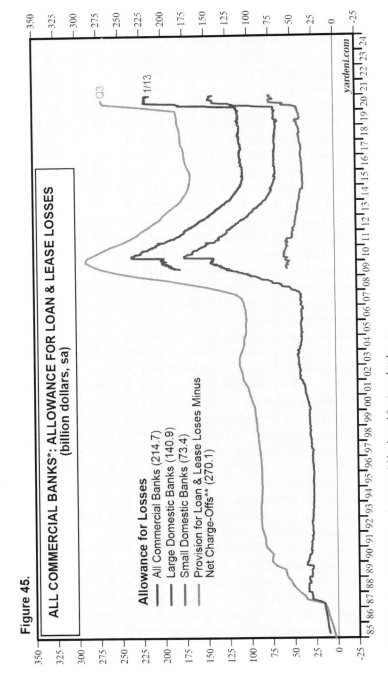

ALL COMMERCIAL BANKS*: ALLOWANCE FOR LOAN & LEASE LOSSES
(billion dollars, sa)

Allowance for Losses
— All Commercial Banks (214.7)
— Large Domestic Banks (140.9)
— Small Domestic Banks (73.4)
— Provision for Loan & Lease Loses Minus
  Net Charge-Offs** (270.1)

* Includes domestically chartered commercial banks and foreign-related ones.
  Cumulative change since 1984. All FDIC-insured financial institutions.
** Source: Federal Reserve Board and Federal Deposit Insurance Corporation, Quarterly Banking Profile.

yardeni.com

Figure 46.

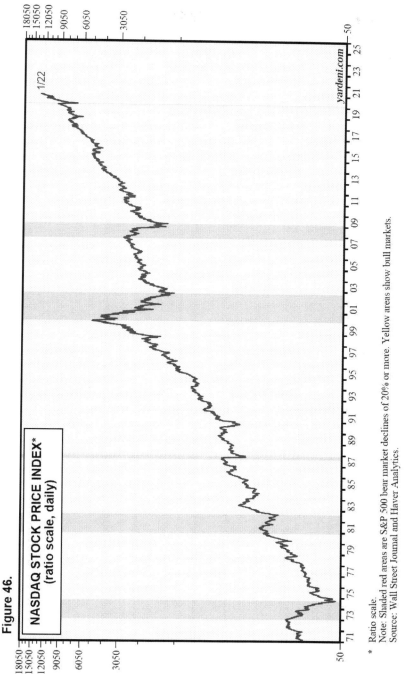

NASDAQ STOCK PRICE INDEX*
(ratio scale, daily)

1/22

yardeni.com

* Ratio scale.
Note: Shaded red areas are S&P 500 bear market declines of 20% or more. Yellow areas show bull markets.
Source: Wall Street Journal and Haver Analytics.

Figure 47.

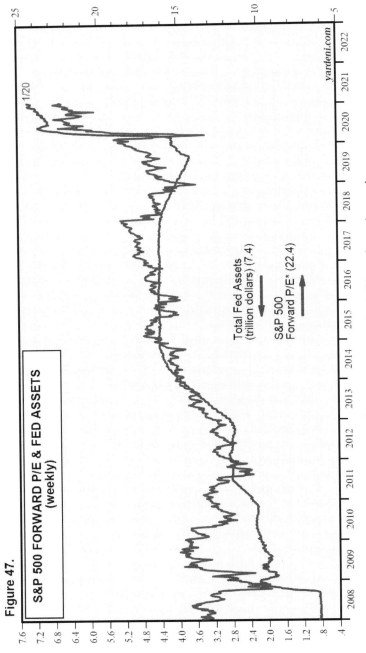

S&P 500 FORWARD P/E & FED ASSETS
(weekly)

Total Fed Assets
(trillion dollars) (7.4)

S&P 500
Forward P/E* (22.4)

yardeni.com

* S&P 500 index divided by year-ahead forward analysts' consensus expected S&P 500 operating earnings per share.
Source: Federal Reserve Board, I/B/E/S data by Refinitiv, and Standard & Poor's.

Figure 48.

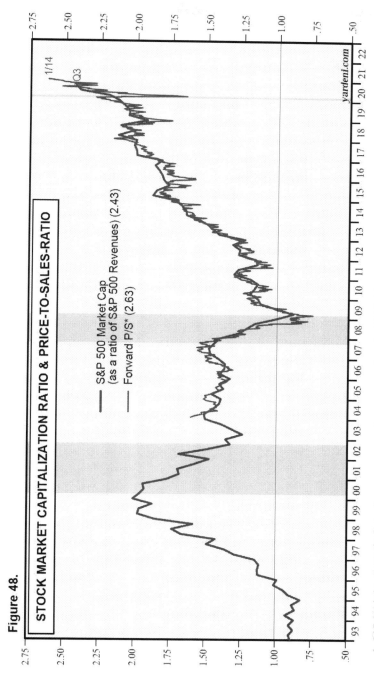

STOCK MARKET CAPITALIZATION RATIO & PRICE-TO-SALES-RATIO

— S&P 500 Market Cap
   (as a ratio of S&P 500 Revenues) (2.43)

— Forward P/S* (2.63)

* S&P 500 index divided by forward consensus expected revenues per share for S&P 500. Monthly through 2005, then weekly.
Note: Shaded red areas are S&P 500 bear market declines of 20% or more. Yellow areas are bull markets.
Source: I/B/E/S data by Refinitiv and Standard & Poor's.

yardeni.com

Notes

Introduction

1. Edward Yardeni, *Fed Watching for Fun and Profit* (2020).
   https://www.amazon.com/gp/product/B085WH9Q6Y/
2. *Fed Watching*, p. 207. I also observed: "In any event, her comment is reminiscent of other ill-fated predictions by Fed chairs—like Greenspan's 'once-in-a-century' technology and productivity revolution and Bernanke's no 'significant spillovers' stance on the subprime mortgage debacle."
3. Liz McCormick, "Jerome Powell Says the Concept of MMT Is 'Just Wrong'," Bloomberg, February 26, 2019.
   https://www.bloomberg.com/news/articles/2019-02-26/
   jay-powell-is-no-fan-of-mmt-says-the-concept-is-just-wrong

Chapter 1

4. Since the December 16, 2020 meeting of the FOMC, the Fed started releasing the SEP at the same time as the FOMC statement. Included in the SEP are two new exhibits that show how the balance of participants' assessments of uncertainty and risks have evolved over time. Previously, the SEP was made available to the public as an addendum to the Minutes that are released three weeks after each meeting.
5. "Nothing to Fear But Nothing to Fear (and Iran)," *Morning Briefing*, January 6, 2020. http://www.yardeni.com/pub/mb_200106.pdf.
6. Ben Bernanke, "The new tools of monetary policy," January 4, 2020 speech. https://www.brookings.edu/blog/ben-bernanke/2020/01/04/
   the-new-tools-of-monetary-policy/
7. See the video at https://www.youtube.com/watch?v=okAIf5-BDAQ.
8. "Summers Calls Bernanke Speech 'Last Hurrah' for Central Bankers," Bloomberg, January 9, 2020.

https://www.bloomberg.com/news/articles/2020-01-09/summers-calls-bernanke-speech-last-hurrah-for-central-bankers

9. Minutes of the Federal Open Market Committee, December 10–11, 2019. https://www.federalreserve.gov/monetarypolicy/files/fomcminutes20191211.pdf

10. Transcript of Chair Powell's Press Conference, December 11, 2019. https://www.federalreserve.gov/mediacenter/files/FOMCpresconf20191211.pdf

11. "Happy Chinese New Year," *Morning Briefing*, January 22, 2020. https://www.yardeni.com/pub/mb_200122.pdf.

12. "Going Viral," *Morning Briefing*, January 27, 2020. https://www.yardeni.com/pub/mb_200127.pdf.

13. "CDC expects 'community spread' of coronavirus, as top official warns disruptions could be 'severe'," STAT, February 25, 2020. https://www.statnews.com/2020/02/25/cdc-expects-community-spread-of-coronavirus-as-top-official-warns-disruptions-could-be-severe/

14. "Where Is Everybody?" *The Twilight Zone*, October 5, 1959 video episode. https://www.paramountplus.com/shows/the-twilight-zone-classic/video/rkp0zUJrpmF29FTeRO_sMN9SGSmLL5Hh/the-twilight-zone-where-is-everybody-/

15. "Government Measures to Stop Covid-19 Triggering Pandemic of Fear," *Morning Briefing*, February 26, 2020. http://www.yardeni.com/pub/mb_200226.pdf.

16. "Pandemic Pandemonium," *Morning Briefing*, March 10, 2020. http://www.yardeni.com/pub/mb_200310.pdf.

17. "The Best Cure for a Viral Pandemic Is a Viral Panic," *Morning Briefing*, March 16, 2020. http://www.yardeni.com/pub/mb_200316.pdf.

Chapter 2

18. "In a Good Place?" *Morning Briefing*, February 19, 2020. https://www.yardeni.com/pub/mb_200219.pdf.

19. Monetary Policy Report, Board of Governors of the Federal Reserve System, February 7, 2020. https://www.federalreserve.gov/monetarypolicy/files/20200207_mprfullreport.pdf

20. Jerome Powell, Semiannual Monetary Policy Report to the Congress, February 11, 2020. https://www.federalreserve.gov/newsevents/testimony/powell20200211a.htm

21. Transcript of Chairman Powell's Press Conference, September 26, 2018. https://www.federalreserve.gov/mediacenter/files/FOMCpresconf20180926.pdf

22. Transcript of Chairman Powell's Press Conference, January 30, 2019. https://www.federalreserve.gov/mediacenter/files/FOMCpresconf20190130.pdf

23. Transcript of Chair Powell's Press Conference, March 20, 2019. https://www.federalreserve.gov/mediacenter/files/FOMCpresconf20190320.pdf

24. Transcript of Chair Powell's Press Conference, January 29, 2020. https://www.federalreserve.gov/mediacenter/files/FOMCpresconf20200129.pdf

25. Jeff Cox, "Fed Vice Chair Clarida throws cold water on traders pricing in a rate cut," CNBC, February 20, 2020. https://www.cnbc.com/2020/02/20/clarida-on-squawk-.html

26. "Statement from Federal Reserve Chair Jerome H. Powell," press release, February 28, 2020. https://www.federalreserve.gov/newsevents/pressreleases/other20200228a.htm

27. "Covid-19: The Plot Sickens," *Morning Briefing*, March 2, 2020. https://www.yardeni.com/pub/mb_200302.pdf.

28. FOMC Statement, March 3, 2020. https://www.federalreserve.gov/monetarypolicy/files/monetary20200303a1.pdf

29. "Fed's Rosengren: Fed Needs to Broaden Assets It Can Buy," *The Wall Street Journal*, March 6, 2020. https://www.wsj.com/articles/fed-s-rosengren-fed-needs-to-broaden-what-assets-it-can-buy-11583515431

30. "Fear for All," *Morning Briefing*, March 12, 2020. https://www.yardeni.com/pub/mb_200312.pdf.

31. Federal Reserve Actions to Support the Flow of Credit to Households and Businesses, Board of Governors of the Federal Reserve System, March 15, 2020. https://www.federalreserve.gov/newsevents/pressreleases/monetary20200315b.htm

32. See our Chronology of Fed's Quantitative Easing & Tightening at www.yardeni.com/chronology-of-feds-quantitative-easing/.

33. FOMC Statement, March 15, 2020. https://www.federalreserve.gov/
monetarypolicy/files/monetary20200315a1.pdf

34. Coordinated Central Bank Action to Enhance the Provision of U.S.
Dollar Liquidity, Board of Governors of the Federal Reserve System,
March 15, 2020. https://www.federalreserve.gov/newsevents/
pressreleases/monetary20200315c.htm

35. "False coronavirus rumors surge in 'hidden viral' text messages," NBC
News, March 16, 2020. https://www.nbcnews.com/tech/tech-news/
false-coronavirus-rumors-surge-hidden-viral-text-messages-n1160936

36. "Declaration of War," *Morning Briefing*, March 17, 2020. http://www.
yardeni.com/pub/mb_200317.pdf.

37. Federal Reserve Board announces establishment of a Primary Dealer
Credit Facility (PDCF) to support the credit needs of households
and businesses, Board of Governors of the Federal Reserve System,
Press Release, March 17, 2020. https://www.federalreserve.gov/
newsevents/pressreleases/monetary20200317b.htm

38. Federal Reserve Board announces establishment of a Commercial
Paper Funding Facility (CPFF) to support the flow of credit to
households and businesses, Board of Governors of the Federal
Reserve System, Press Release, March 17, 2020. https://www.
federalreserve.gov/newsevents/pressreleases/monetary20200317a.htm

39. Federal Reserve Board broadens program of support for the flow of
credit to households and businesses by establishing a Money Market
Mutual Fund Liquidity Facility (MMLF), Board of Governors of the
Federal Reserve System, Press Release, March 18, 2020. https://www.
federalreserve.gov/newsevents/pressreleases/monetary20200318a.htm

40. Federal Reserve Board expands its program of support for flow
of credit to the economy by taking steps to enhance liquidity and
functioning of crucial state and municipal money markets, Board of
Governors of the Federal Reserve System, Press Release, March 20,
2020. https://www.federalreserve.gov/newsevents/pressreleases/
monetary20200320b.htm

41. "Declaration of War," *Morning Briefing*, March 17, 2020. https://www.
yardeni.com/pub/mb_200317.pdf.

42. "Searching for Silver Bullets," *Morning Briefing*, March 25, 2020.
https://www.yardeni.com/pub/mb_200325.pdf.

43. Federal Reserve announces extensive new measures to support the economy, Board of Governors of the Federal Reserve System, Press Release, March 23, 2020. https://www.federalreserve.gov/newsevents/pressreleases/monetary20200323b.htm

44. "Federal Reserve Considering Additional Support for State, Local Government Finance," *The Wall Street Journal*, March 27, 2020. https://www.wsj.com/articles/federal-reserve-considering-additional-support-for-state-and-local-government-finance-11585335550?mod=hp_lead_pos7

45. Federal Reserve takes additional actions to provide up to $2.3 trillion in loans to support the economy, Board of Governors of the Federal Reserve System, Press Release, April 9, 2020. https://www.federalreserve.gov/newsevents/pressreleases/monetary20200409a.htm

46. Federal Reserve Board announces an extension through December 31 of its lending facilities that were scheduled to expire on or around September 30, Board of Governors of the Federal Reserve System, Press Release, July 28, 2020. https://www.federalreserve.gov/newsevents/pressreleases/monetary20200728a.htm

47. Federal Reserve Board announces extension through March 31, 2021, for several of its lending facilities that were generally scheduled to expire on or around December 31, Board of Governors of the Federal Reserve System, Press Release, November 30, 2020. https://www.federalreserve.gov/newsevents/pressreleases/monetary20201130a.htm

48. FOMC Statement, December 16, 2020. https://www.federalreserve.gov/monetarypolicy/files/monetary20201216a1.pdf

49. See our handy archive of FOMC Statements 1997–Present at https://www.yardeni.com/fed-center/.

50. "Fed Chair Jay Powell: U.S. may be in a different era for workers' wages despite economic gains," PBS NewsHour (pbs.org), October 3, 2018. Quoted remark is 11 minutes, 17 seconds into the videotape of the interview. https://www.pbs.org/newshour/show/fed-chair-jay-powell-u-s-may-be-in-a-different-era-for-workers-wages-despite-economic-gains

51. Transcript of Chair Powell's Press Conference, March 3, 2020. https://www.federalreserve.gov/mediacenter/files/FOMCpresconf20200303.pdf

52. "Transcript of Chair Powell's Press Conference Call," March 15, 2020. https://www.federalreserve.gov/mediacenter/files/ FOMCpresconf20200315.pdf

53. "Transcript of Chair Powell's Press Conference," April 29, 2020. https://www.federalreserve.gov/mediacenter/files/ FOMCpresconf20200429.pdf

54. "Full Transcript: Fed Chair Jerome Powell's 60 Minutes Interview on Economic Recovery From the Coronavirus Pandemic," May 17, 2020. https://www.cbsnews.com/news/full-transcript-fed-chair-jerome-powell-60-minutes-interview-economic-recovery-from-coronavirus-pandemic/

55. "Powell Says Fed Crossed Red Lines When Virus Demanded Action," Bloomberg, May 29, 2020. https:// www.bloomberg.com/news/articles/2020-05-29/ powell-says-fed-crossed-red-lines-because-virus-demanded-action

56. "Transcript of Chair Powell's Press Conference," June 10, 2020. https://www.federalreserve.gov/mediacenter/files/ FOMCpresconf20200610.pdf

57. "Transcript of Chair Powell's Press Conference," July 29, 2020. https://www.federalreserve.gov/mediacenter/files/ FOMCpresconf20200729.pdf

58. "Transcript of Chair Powell's Press Conference," September 16, 2020. https://www.federalreserve.gov/mediacenter/files/ FOMCpresconf20200916.pdf

59. Jerome Powell, "Recent Economic Developments and the Challenges Ahead," October 6, 2020 speech at the National Association for Business Economics Virtual Annual Meeting. https://www.federalreserve.gov/newsevents/speech/ powell20201006a.htm

60. "The Fiscal Federal Reserve: Powell signs up to monetize trillions of dollars in more spending," *The Wall Street Journal*, October 7, 2020. https://www.wsj.com/articles/the-fiscal-federal-reserve-11602112823

61. "Preliminary Estimate of the Effects of H.R. 748, the CARES Act," Congressional Budget Office, April 27, 2020. https://www.cbo.gov/ system/files/2020-04/hr748.pdf

62. "Don't Fight T-Fed," *Morning Briefing*, October 12, 2020. https://www. yardeni.com/pub/mb_201012.pdf.

63. Transcript of Chair Powell's Press Conference, June 10, 2020. https://www.federalreserve.gov/mediacenter/files/ FOMCpresconf20200610.pdf

64. Transcript of Chair Powell's Press Conference, July 29, 2020. https://www.federalreserve.gov/mediacenter/files/ FOMCpresconf20200729.pdf

65. Minutes of the Federal Open Market Committee, June 9–10, 2020. https://www.federalreserve.gov/monetarypolicy/files/ fomcminutes20200610.pdf

Chapter 3

66. "ECB ready to take 'appropriate and targeted measures' on coronavirus," *Financial Times*, March 2, 2020. https://www.ft.com/content/98fb0c6a-5cd4-11ea-b0ab-339c2307bcd4

67. ECB, Monetary policy decisions, March 12, 2020. https://www.ecb.europa.eu/press/pr/date/2020/html/ecb. mp200312~8d3aec3ff2.en.html

68. ECB announces easing of conditions for targeted longer-term refinancing operations (TLTRO III), ECB Press Release, March 12, 2020. https://www.ecb.europa.eu/press/pr/date/2020/html/ecb. pr200312_1~39db50b717.en.html

69. Press Conference, ECB, 12 March 2020. https://www.ecb.europa.eu/ press/pressconf/2020/html/ecb.is200312~f857a21b6c.en.html

70. ECB announces €750 billion Pandemic Emergency Purchase Programme (PEPP), ECB Press Release, March 18, 2020. https://www.ecb.europa.eu/press/pr/date/2020/html/ecb. pr200318_1~3949d6f266.en.html

71. ECB, Monetary policy decisions, June 4, 2020. https://www.ecb. europa.eu/press/pr/date/2020/html/ecb.mp200604~a307d3429c. en.html

72. ECB announces new pandemic emergency longer-term refinancing operations, April 30, 2020. https://www.ecb.europa.eu/press/pr/ date/2020/html/ecb.pr200430_1~477f400e39.en.html

73. ECB, Monetary policy decisions, December 10, 2020. https://www.ecb.europa.eu/press/pr/date/2020/html/ecb.mp201210~8c2778b843.en.html. ECB extends pandemic emergency longer-term refinancing operations, Press Release, December 10, 2020. https://www.ecb.europa.eu/press/pr/date/2020/html/ecb.pr201210~8acfa5026f.en.html

74. Christine Lagarde, "Europe's response to the crisis," ECB Blog Post, July 23, 2020. https://www.ecb.europa.eu/press/blog/date/2020/html/ecb.blog200723~c06fafabb6.en.html

75. "Economic and monetary developments," ECB *Economic Bulletin*, September 24, 2020. https://www.ecb.europa.eu/pub/economic-bulletin/html/eb202006.en.html#toc1

76. "Lagarde Is Prepared to Add Stimulus, Cut Rates to Support European Recovery," *The Wall Street Journal*, October 6, 2020. https://www.wsj.com/articles/ecbs-christine-lagarde-is-prepared-to-inject-fresh-stimulus-cut-rates-11601973358

77. Enhancement of Monetary Easing in Light of the Impact of the Outbreak of the Novel Coronavirus (COVID-19), Monetary Policy Release, Bank of Japan, March 16, 2020. https://www.boj.or.jp/en/announcements/release_2020/k200316b.pdf

78. "Japan Unveils Record $992 Billion Stimulus Amid Virus Emergency," Bloomberg, April 7, 2020. https://www.bloomberg.com/news/articles/2020-04-07/japan-readies-extra-16-8-trillion-yen-to-fund-record-stimulus

79. Enhancement of Monetary Easing, Monetary Policy Release, Bank of Japan, April 27, 2020. https://www.boj.or.jp/en/mopo/mpmdeci/state_2020/k200427a.htm/

80. "Japan approves fresh $1.1 trillion stimulus to combat pandemic pain," Reuters, May 26, 2020. https://www.reuters.com/article/us-health-coronavirus-japan-stimulus/japan-approves-fresh-1-1-trillion-stimulus-to-combat-pandemic-pain-idUSKBN2323D3

81. "To fight pandemic, Japan keeps fiscal tap wide open on budget spending requests," *The Japan Times*, July 21, 2020. https://www.japantimes.co.jp/news/2020/07/21/business/economy-business/japan-budget-spending-requests-coronavirus/

Chapter 4

82. "CBO's Current Projections of Output, Employment, and Interest Rates and a Preliminary Look at Federal Deficits for 2020 and 2021," Congressional Budget Office (cbo.gov), April 24, 2020. https://www.cbo.gov/publication/56335

83. "Awakenings," *Morning Briefing*, May 18, 2020. https://www.yardeni.com/pub/mb_200518.pdf.

84. "From Cabin Fever to Dopamine Rush," *Morning Briefing*, May 21, 2020. https://www.yardeni.com/pub/mb_200521.pdf.

85. Sandy Cohan and Edward Yardeni, "Cabin Fever Sing Along," April 27, 2020. https://www.linkedin.com/pulse/cabin-fever-sing-a-long-edward-yardeni/

86. GAFO stands for general merchandise, apparel and accessories, furniture and furnishings, and other—representing retailers of department-store types of merchandise (e.g., furniture and home furnishings, electronics and appliances, clothing and accessories, sporting goods, hobby, musical instrument, and book, general merchandise, office supply, stationery, and gift stores).

87. "How are the economic impact payments for individuals authorized by the CARES Act of 2020 recorded in the NIPAs?" Bureau of Economic Analysis, April 28, 2020. https://www.bea.gov/help/faq/1409

88. "Moderna Announces Positive Interim Phase 1 Data for its mRNA Vaccine (mRNA-1273) Against Novel Coronavirus," Press Release, Moderna, Inc., May 18, 2020. https://investors.modernatx.com/news-releases/news-release-details/moderna-announces-positive-interim-phase-1-data-its-mrna-vaccine

Chapter 5

89. Jerome Powell, "New Economic Challenges and the Fed's Monetary Policy Review," August 27, 2020 speech at "Navigating the Decade Ahead: Implications for Monetary Policy," an economic policy symposium sponsored by the Federal Reserve Bank of Kansas City, Jackson Hole, Wyoming (via webcast). https://www.federalreserve.gov/newsevents/speech/powell20200827a.htm

90. "Federal Reserve issues FOMC statement of longer-run goals and policy strategy," Press Release, January 25, 2012. https://www.federalreserve.gov/newsevents/pressreleases/monetary20120125c.htm

91. "Statement on Longer-Run Goals and Monetary Policy Strategy," Adopted effective January 24, 2012; as amended effective August 27, 2020. https://www.federalreserve.gov/monetarypolicy/review-of-monetary-policy-strategy-tools-and-communications-statement-on-longer-run-goals-monetary-policy-strategy.htm

92. "Guide to changes in the Statement on Longer-Run Goals and Monetary Policy Strategy," Board of Governors of the Federal Reserve System, August 27, 2020. https://www.federalreserve.gov/monetarypolicy/guide-to-changes-in-statement-on-longer-run-goals-monetary-policy-strategy.htm

93. Lael Brainard, "Bringing the Statement on Longer-Run Goals and Monetary Policy Strategy into Alignment with Longer-Run Changes in the Economy," September 1, 2020 speech at "How the Fed Will Respond to the COVID-19 Recession in an Era of Low Rates and Low Inflation," an event hosted by the Hutchins Center on Fiscal and Monetary Policy at the Brookings Institution, Washington, D.C. (via webcast). https://www.federalreserve.gov/newsevents/speech/brainard20200901a.htm

94. "Timelines of Policy Actions and Communications: Statement on Longer-Run Goals and Monetary Policy Strategy," February 22, 2019, Board of Governors of the Federal Reserve System. https://www.federalreserve.gov/monetarypolicy/timeline-statement-on-longer-run-goals-and-monetary-policy-strategy.htm

95. Edward Yardeni, *Four Deflationary Forces Keeping a Lid on Inflation*, Excerpt from *Fed Watching for Fun & Profit* (2020). http://www.yardeni.com/pub/mb_200518_excerpt.pdf

96. Janet Yellen, "Macroeconomic Research After the Crisis," October 14, 2016 speech at "The Elusive 'Great' Recovery: Causes and Implications for Future Business Cycle Dynamics" 60th annual economic conference sponsored by the Federal Reserve Bank of Boston, Boston, Massachusetts. https://www.federalreserve.gov/newsevents/speech/yellen20161014a.htm

Chapter 6

97. See the transcript of Martin's "Address before the New York Group of the Investment Bankers Association of America," October 19, 1955. https://fraser.stlouisfed.org/title/statements-speeches-william-mcchesney-martin-jr-448/address-new-york-group-investment-bankers-association-america-7800

98. Aaron Steelman. "Employment Act of 1946," Federal Reserve History webpage. https://www.federalreservehistory.org/essays/employment-act-of-1946

99. *Financial Stability Report*, Board of Governors of the Federal Reserve System, November 2018. https://www.federalreserve.gov/publications/files/financial-stability-report-201811.pdf

100. *Financial Stability Report*, Board of Governors of the Federal Reserve System, May 2019. https://www.federalreserve.gov/publications/files/financial-stability-report-201905.pdf

101. *Financial Stability Report*, Board of Governors of the Federal Reserve System, November 2019. https://www.federalreserve.gov/publications/files/financial-stability-report-20191115.pdf

102. *Global Financial Stability Report*, International Monetary Fund, October 2019. https://www.imf.org/-/media/Files/Publications/GFSR/2019/October/English/text.ashx

103. "Transcript of Chair Powell's Press Conference," October 30, 2019. https://www.federalreserve.gov/mediacenter/files/FOMCpresconf20191030.pdf

104. *Financial Stability Report*, Board of Governors of the Federal Reserve System, May 2020. https://www.federalreserve.gov/publications/files/financial-stability-report-20200515.pdf

105. *Financial Stability Report*, Board of Governors of the Federal Reserve System, November 2020. https://www.federalreserve.gov/publications/files/financial-stability-report-20201109.pdf

106. "Dodd-Frank Act Stress Test 2020: Supervisory Stress Test Results," Federal Reserve Board of Governors of the Federal Reserve System, June 2020. https://www.federalreserve.gov/publications/files/2020-dfast-results-20200625.pdf, Federal Reserve Board releases results of stress tests for 2020 and additional sensitivity analyses conducted in light of the coronavirus event, Federal Reserve Board of Governors

of the Federal Reserve System, Press Release, June 25, 2020. https://www.federalreserve.gov/newsevents/pressreleases/bcreg20200625c.htm

107. Statement by Governor Brainard, Federal Reserve Board of Governors of the Federal Reserve System, Press release, June 25, 2020. https://www.federalreserve.gov/newsevents/pressreleases/brainard-statement-20200625c.htm

108. Federal Reserve Board announces it will extend for an additional quarter several measures to ensure that large banks maintain a high level of capital resilience, Federal Reserve Board of Governors of the Federal Reserve System, Press release, September 30, 2020. https://www.federalreserve.gov/newsevents/pressreleases/bcreg20200930b.htm

109. *December 2020 Stress Test Results*, Federal Reserve Board of Governors of the Federal Reserve System. https://www.federalreserve.gov/publications/files/2020-dec-stress-test-results-20201218.pdf

110. Federal Reserve Board releases second round of bank stress test results, Federal Reserve Board of Governors of the Federal Reserve System, Press release, December 18, 2020. https://www.federalreserve.gov/newsevents/pressreleases/bcreg20201218b.htm

111. Executive Order 12631 — Working Group on Financial Markets, Ronald Reagan Presidential Library & Museum. https://www.reaganlibrary.gov/archives/speech/executive-order-12631-working-group-financial-markets

112. "Plunge Protection Team," *The Washington Post*, February 23, 1997. https://www.washingtonpost.com/wp-srv/business/longterm/blackm/plunge.htm

113. "The Three Marketeers," *Time*, February 15, 1999. http://content.time.com/time/world/article/0,8599,2054093,00.html

114. *Global Financial Stability Report*, International Monetary Fund, October 2020. https://www.imf.org/-/media/Files/Publications/GFSR/2019/October/English/text.ashx

115. Nick Timiraos, "Mnuchin, Powell Pledge Additional Relief to Prevent Lasting Damage to Economy," *The Wall Street Journal*, June 30, 2020. https://www.wsj.com/articles/fed-chairman-says-economy-faces-new-challenges-from-coronavirus-11593516603

116. "Periodic Report: Update on Outstanding Lending Facilities Authorized by the Board under Section 13(3) of the Federal Reserve Act December 10, 2020," Federal Reserve Board of Governors. https://www.federalreserve.gov/publications/files/pdcf-mmlf-cpff-pmccf-smccf-talf-mlf-ppplf-msnlf-mself-msplf-nonlf-noelf-12-11-20.pdf

117. Treasury Secretary Steven Mnuchin's letter to Fed Chair Jerome Powell, November 19, 2020. https://home.treasury.gov/system/files/136/letter11192020.pdf

118. Parinitha Sastry, "The Political Origins of Section 13(3) of the Federal Reserve Act," *FRBNY Economic Policy Review*, September 2018. https://www.newyorkfed.org/medialibrary/media/research/epr/2018/epr_2018_political-origins_sastry.pdf

119. Jeanna Smialek, "What Is 13-3? Why a Debate Over the Fed Is Holding Up Stimulus Talks," *The New York Times*, December 18, 2020. https://www.nytimes.com/2020/12/18/business/economy/fed-13-3-stimulus.html?searchResultPosition=8

120. The Fed extended these four facilities through March 31, 2021. See: Federal Reserve Board announces extension through March 31, 2021, for several of its lending facilities that were generally scheduled to expire on or around December 31, Board of Governors of the Federal Reserve System, Press Release, November 30, 2020. https://www.federalreserve.gov/newsevents/pressreleases/monetary20201130a.htm

121. Letter from Chair Powell to Secretary Mnuchin regarding emergency lending facilities, Board of Governors of the Federal Reserve System, November 20, 2020. https://www.federalreserve.gov/foia/letter-from-chair-powell-to-secretary-mnuchin-20201120.htm

122. "Pandemic increases risks to financial stability," ECB Press Release. https://www.ecb.europa.eu/press/pr/date/2020/html/ecb.pr200526~cbbd04bd5d.en.html, *Financial Stability Report*, ECB, May 2020. https://www.ecb.europa.eu/pub/financial-stability/fsr/html/ecb.fsr201911~facad0251f.en.html#toc1

123. *Financial Stability Report*, Federal Reserve Board of the Federal Reserve System, November 2020. https://www.federalreserve.gov/publications/files/financial-stability-report-20201109.pdf

124. Transcript of Chair Powell's Press Conference, December 16, 2020. https://www.federalreserve.gov/mediacenter/files/ FOMCpresconf20201216.pdf

125. Alan Greenspan, "The Challenge of Central Banking in a Democratic Society," December 5, 1996 speech at the Annual Dinner and Francis Boyer Lecture of The American Enterprise Institute for Public Policy Research, Washington, D.C. https://www.federalreserve.gov/ boarddocs/speeches/1996/19961205.htm

126. For a thorough explanation of forward revenues, forward earnings, forward P/Es, and the Buffett Ratio see Edward Yardeni and Joseph Abbott, *S&P 500 Earnings, Valuation, and the Pandemic*, 2020. https://www.amazon.com/gp/product/B08NXYYVHQ/

127. Jerome Powell, "Thoughts on Unconventional Monetary Policy," June 27, 2013 speech at the Bipartisan Policy Center, Washington, D.C. https://www.federalreserve.gov/newsevents/speech/ powell20130627a.htm

Chapter 7

128. Stephanie Kelton, *The Deficit Myth: Modern Monetary Theory and the Birth of the People's Economy* (New York: PublicAffairs, 2020), page 13. https://www.amazon.com/dp/B07RM72BT7/

129. Kelton, page 17.

130. Kelton, page 63.

131. Kelton, page 96.

132. Kelton, page 134.

133. Kelton, page 22.

134. Kelton, page 38.

135. Kelton, page 237.

136. Kelton, pages 33-34.

137. Kelton, page 56.

138. Kelton, page 65.

139. Kelton, page 249.

Epilogue

140. "A Conversation with Federal Reserve Chair Jerome Powell," Bendheim Center for Finance, Princeton University,

January 14, 2021. See the video at https://bcf.princeton.edu/news/a-conversation-with-federal-reserve-chair-jerome-powell/.

141. "Biden Proposes $1.9 Trillion Covid-19 Relief Package," Richard Rubin and Eliza Collins, *The Wall Street Journal*, January 14, 2021. https://www.wsj.com/articles/biden-to-propose-1-9-trillion-covid-19-package-11610661977

142. "Fed's Rosengren voices support for Biden stimulus proposal," Jeff Cox, CNBC.com, January 15, 2021. https://www.cnbc.com/2021/01/15/fed-rosengren-voices-support-for-biden-stimulus-proposal.html

143. Federal Reserve issues FOMC statement, Press Release, December 16, 2020. https://www.federalreserve.gov/newsevents/pressreleases/monetary20201216a.htm

Made in the USA
Middletown, DE
19 August 2023

36978258R10106